Free Spirits

Irish Travellers and Irish Traditional Music

TOMMY FEGAN

OLIVER O'CONNELL

Layout: Mark Larkin
Design: Irene McGinn
Printed by Clanrye Press, Newry, Co Down

ISBN 978-0-9570194-0-9 (Paperback)

"The European Agricultural Fund for Rural Development: Europe investing in rural areas"
The publishers acknowledge the financial support for this publication from Clare Local Development Company through LEADER RDP.

Dedicated to the memory of

Kevin Fegan and Maureen O'Connell

Travevller family inside a shelter tent. (Courtesy of The Navan Travellers Workshops)

Preface

Our lifelong involvement in Irish traditional music, and our shared love and appreciation of the music of Irish Traveller families, led to our paths crossing for the first time at the inaugural Doran Tionól in Wicklow in 2000. The event was organised by Wicklow piper Dinny Quigley, Dick Barton and Terry Murphy to celebrate the music legacy of Johnny and Felix Doran, two Traveller brothers who were legendary uilleann pipers in the first half of the 20th century. Over the following eight years, we developed a strong friendship with the Doran extended family and, in April 2008 at the 9th Doran Tionól in Spanish Point, Co Clare, we came to the conclusion that the story of Johnny and Felix Doran should be fully documented and made available. Having decided to write the story of the two famous Doran brothers, we quickly concluded that theirs is only part of a wider story about the role of Irish Travellers and their impact on Irish traditional music over the last three centuries.

Since then, we have embarked on a journey that has touched and humbled us as we gained the confidence and respect of many of the most influential Traveller musicians of the past century. We were invited into a world that we knew existed, but was off limits, and we are grateful to all our friends in the Traveller community for allowing us into their musical life so that this book could become a reality.

There are currently 40,000 Irish Travellers in Ireland, 15,000 in the United Kingdom, and a further 12,000 Travellers of Irish descent living in the United States of America. One of the key characteristics of Irish Travellers is their nomadic lifestyle, and many of them earned their livelihood from bringing much-needed services - repairing tin buckets, cans and other household utensils which were then predominantly made from tin-to rural parts of Ireland for centuries. The rapid pace of new technologies, the availability of cheap goods, access to better communications and other developments in the 1950s heralded major changes in Irish Travellers' lifestyles.

A small number of Irish Travellers had become expert exponents of Irish traditional music, particularly on the uilleann pipes and fiddle. Although they were small in number, they had a major influence on the broader world of Irish traditional music and their impact has never been fully documented until now.

We wish to acknowledge the endorsement of all the Traveller families who are the subject of this book. We have enjoyed their hospitality, their advice and, equally important, their friendship.

Irish traditional music is enjoying unprecedented popularity globally, as is manifest by the growing audiences for performances or recordings of Riverdance, Lord of the Dance, the Chieftains, the Fureys, Planxty, the Bothy Band and many others. This book will demonstrate that Irish Travellers made a direct and significant contribution to the music that currently underpins this 21st century phenomenon. The uilleann pipes in particular have been central to this sound. Bands and groups that have been to the fore in the globalisation of Irish traditional music in the 20th century, all featured the uilleann pipes at the heart of their respective sounds.

We owe it to them now to acknowledge their contribution to Irish culture.

The Traveller families involved in this story were very anxious that the details of this extraordinary way of life and musical legacy be recorded, and made public, before it is too late. We believe that this story will be particularly relevant in a post-Celtic Tiger era that places more value on Irish cultural heritage, at home and abroad.

Ireland and Irish culture is richer because of the music and songs of the Traveller community, who for centuries were one of the few means of entertainment throughout rural Ireland. Wherever Irish music is played, wherever Irish songs are sung, wherever Irish stories are told and wherever Irish dances are performed, the influences of the Dorans, the Keenans, the Fureys, the Dunnes, the Dohertys and other great Traveller musical families will be very much in evidence.

"Thank you for the friendship and the music".

Tommy Fegan   *Oliver O'Connell*

Acknowledgements:

Producing this publication has been an extraordinary journey for the authors, as we came into contact with some of the most interesting and memorable people we have ever met. We would like to thank the following people who made this book a reality.

We are indebted to Muiris O'Rocháin, a remarkable man who has done so much for Irish culture, Harry Hughes; Michael Falsey; Paddy O'Donoughue; Sean Talty; Leo Rickard; Jeremiah Dunne; Christy Dunne; and the late John Joe Dunne for their contributions and encouragement to us in this endeavour.

To Paddy Keenan, his brother Thomas, and to the family of the late Johnny Keenan, thank you so much for such a legacy.
We want to say a special word of thanks to Mickey and Aideen Dunne, and their two daughters Bríd and Niamh who are carrying the musical flag for the next generation. Mickey was so helpful and informative on this subject, and Aideen cast a valuable eye on its journey to publication.

We thank the maestro himself, Finbar Furey, who played for us, sang for us, told us stories and made us laugh and cry with his vast knowledge of Irish music and his undoubted comic genius. We are also indebted to him for giving us the book's title - *Free Spirits* - which encapsulates this powerful story better than anything we could imagine.

To the Doran families in England, Mikey Doran Sr, his wife Marie, and their family; Mikey Doran Jr, his wife Nan, and son Mikey , all of the Doran siblings and descendants of the legendary Felix Doran, thank you so much for your friendship and hospitality.

To Johnny Doran's daughters, Nan and Eileen, his son Jimmy, to Johnny Purcell, grandson of Johnny Doran to Bridget (Cash) Purcell, thank you for your help and encouragement and for your confidence in us. We hope you are pleased and proud of the end result.

We want to say a special thank you to John and Bridgie Rooney and their son Larry Rooney who helped us on our way. Special thanks also to William Dundon and to Simon Doyle and his talented family.

To the staff of Na Píobairí Uilleann, the Irish Folklore Commission UCD, Pavee Point, the Irish Traditional Music Archive, Siobhán Ní Chorain and Comhaltas Ceolteoirí Éireann, Baile Atha Cliath, Clare Library, Mary Connolly and staff at the Tara Education Centre, Co Louth VEC, and Michael McDonagh at the Navan Travellers Workshop, míle buíochas libh go léir.

To Michael O'Connell, Pat Broderick; Joe Doyle, Noel Hill, Josephine Keegan, Rab Cherry, Gerry O'Connor, Alen Mac Weeney, Martin Nolan, Leo Rickard, and Pat Costello, our sincere gratitude. To the members of the Doherty family, Margaret Rainey and Cathleen Gaynor and to the family of Maggie Barry, Co Down, thank you.

A special word of thanks to the Pecker Dunne and his wife Madeline and family in Knockerra, Co Clare. Thank you to Brother Seán McNamara and Ollie and Paul Markham in West Clare. A special thanks and prayer for the late great Gerry Lynch from Kilfenora.

We are grateful to Jesse Smith, Peig Macaufield, Róisín Crumlish and Áine Furey who assisted us with transcriptions and to Na Píobairí Uilleann for permission to reproduce transcriptions of Johnny Doran tunes. These tunes were originally transcribed by Breandán Breathnach, Jackie Small, Seán Donnelly and Terry Moylan. We are indebted to Professor Kieran Taaffe and Dr Siobhán Ní Chonaill Cambridge University, who reviewed earlier drafts of this book and made useful suggestions for improvement.

The research for this book has been greatly assisted by the staff of the Dundalk Institute of Technology, and the Department of Music and Creative Media in particular. We are indebted to Dr Eibhlís Farrell, Dr Helen Lawlor and Eamonn Crudden, for their persistence and insistence on the highest standards; Alphie Mulligan (for the impromptu tune to lift the spirits); Derek Farrell and Paul O'Hale for technical support; Alphie's brothers, Tom and Neilidh and their extended family, for all their encouragement; Mark Larkin and Irene McGinn, two creative media graduates for all this imaginative and detailed design work, and for support in so many other ways. And finally to our families and friends for all their encouragement and help.

Table of Contents

A Note on Irish Travellers

Travellers are an indigenous minority group who, historical sources confirm, have been part of Irish society for centuries. Travellers have a shared history, cultural values, language (Cant or Gammon), customs and traditions that make them a self-defined group, and one which is recognisable and distinct. Their culture and way of life and their unique spirit very much depends on an atmosphere of cultural cohesion and physical freedom which distinguishes them from the sedentary (settled) population. A Traveller comes from an extended network of families. You cannot just decide to become a Traveller. If a non-Traveller marries a Traveller, he or she does not become a Traveller, although their children will.

There are over 40,000 Travellers in Ireland. This constitutes approximately 0.5% of the total national population. It is estimated that an additional 15,000 Irish Travellers live in the United Kingdom, with a further 12,000 Travellers of Irish descent living in the United the States of America.

Travellers, as individuals and as a group, experience high levels of prejudice and exclusion in Irish society. Discrimination and its effects is a daily feature of Travellers' lives. Many families today still have to endure living in intolerable conditions, without access to the basic facilities of sanitation, water and electricity. This leads to ongoing health problems within the Traveller community. A recent report of *The National Traveller Health Study* (2007-2010) revealed that Traveller men live, on average, 15 years less than settled men, while Traveller women live on average 11 ½ years less than their settled peers. Infant mortality is much higher than the national average. Very few Travellers reach old age and currently (2010) there are only 8 Travellers in Ireland over the age of 85. In fact, the life expectancy, outcomes, and living standards of modern Travellers are more comparable with those living in developing nations rather than in a western developed country.

Traveller life of yesteryear and many of the traditions that live on today.

Over the years Travellers have gone through major changes in their lifestyle and the pressures to assimilate. With the change in Travellers' mode of accommodation and the move towards living a more sedentary life, it might be expected that this would compromise the Traveller tradition of ceileing (k-lee-ing). However, while Travellers are less nomadic and no longer live on the roadside, they still congregate each evening with their own and extended family to share their news. At these times, many a singsong would start, creating a feeling of togetherness and warmth, as they recall the precious and colourful life of Travellers in times gone by.

Music has always been vitally important to Travellers as a means of telling stories, entertaining, relaxing and enjoying themselves. The words of songs are listened to in detail and the story and meaning of a song is often discussed. This would have been commonplace as, traditionally, Travellers did not use the written word; songs were adapted and changed to personalise and retain an event in that family's history. Many a famous song had the lyrics changed, sometimes for the better, and the revised version would become more commonplace for Travellers to sing.

Roles of the family

The Traveller family is very much led by the father and everyone has a chore to do. In days gone by, the younger boys collected sticks for the fire and water, while the older boys and the father would attend to the horses and then go 'jobbing' ; looking for work or producing tin for sale. The young girls would help with their younger siblings, dressing, washing and preparing breakfast. The women spent their days 'hawking' or selling their wares (swag, religious pictures, household wares, paper flowers, wild flowers and camphor balls, and perform fortune telling). They would describe what they were doing as 'going off to the country'. Traditionally, male Travellers congregate together for most of their activities and female Travellers and young children would spend the majority of their time together. It would be at these times that stories were told and songs were sung.

In times past, when Travellers were more nomadic and lived on the roadside it was quite rare to find an individual family travelling on their own; it would usually be a group of maybe three families. At several times in the year, Travellers would meet in much larger groups, at fairs, markets or family events such as weddings, funerals and christenings. It was at these times that Travellers would gather around one of the fires and would tell stories of events they had experienced since the last time they met. These stories were both a form of entertainment as well as a means of sharing important information. Some of these stories would have been in song format along with other very traditional and old songs and, in this way, Travellers were very much the guardians of old traditional songs and music. Without this, the world would not have such a vast collection of old songs and stories. Every family would have their singers, and these individuals would be renowned for their repertoire of songs and stories.

Micheal McDonagh
Navan Travellers Workshops
(NTW)

Stokes family from Derry (Courtesy of The Navan Travellers Workshops)

Introduction

Johnny Doran's musical legacy is far reaching, and fully appreciated by those who recognised his genius and the influence he brought to bear, directly and indirectly on the development of Irish traditional music in the 20th century. Today, well-known players, such as Finbar Furey and Paddy Keenan acknowledge the influence his short playing career has had on their own music and, consequently, on the subsequent generations of musicians who have in turn been influenced by them.

Their music, by their own admission, is shaped and styled on Doran's techniques. The Furey Brothers and Davy Arthur, as well as the Bothy Band, used the Doran sound of uilleann pipes to build a fresh, driving, attacking sense of wild abandon that would excite young followers across the world. In turn, new generations of pipers like Davy Spillane and Michael O'Connell from Co Clare, adopted the Doran sound and continue to bring it to new worldwide audiences in their own recordings and performances, and as lead players in Riverdance, Lord of the Dance and other global shows.

Elsewhere in Ireland, families such as the Dohertys in Co Donegal, the Raineys in Connemara, and the Dunnes in Co Limerick and Co Clare exerted a similar influence in the shaping of Irish Traditional music throughout the 20th century. They inherited the music from their parents, grandparents and great grandparents, many of whom are referenced in these pages.

In addition to testimonies from the Traveller family members, the extent to which members of the non-Traveller community paid homage to the influence of Irish Traveller musicians is impressive. We are delighted to record the generous cooperation of the many educational, cultural and artistic organisations that not only made their records and archives available to us, but also welcomed this initiative to shine a light on an extraordinary group of people who did so much for Irish traditional music.

This is the story of the major Traveller families that are associated with the development of Irish Traditional music over the last three centuries. We have also included some other individuals from the Traveller community who made significant and colourful contributions to the story. Time precluded us from doing an even more in depth study of others from the Irish Traveller community who played traditional music.

Opposite Page: Mickey Dunne, John Rooney, Paddy Keenan and Finbar Furey. The Doran Tionól, Spanish Point, Co Clare, 2009. (Courtesy of Leo Rickard)
This Page: The Wicklow Mountains (Courtesy of Joe King)

Chapter 1: The Cashes

John Cash (1832-1906)

John Cash was born in County Wexford in 1832 and spent most of his life playing uilleann pipes as he travelled back and forth between Connemara and Wicklow, buying and selling horses and ponies. He combined his talents for horse dealing and tinsmithing with playing the uilleann pipes to provide a comfortable lifestyle for his wife, the young, attractive and noted dancer, Polly Connors.

Cash learned his music from his uncle James Hanrahan, and so began a great piping dynasty that has given rise to a unique style of piping (the Travellers' style). In the penal times in Ireland under British rule Catholicism was banned, Irish culture was suppressed, Irish games were outlawed, and priests who were found saying mass were persecuted. Irish musicians - fiddlers, flautists and harpers - were jailed. Pipers were executed as the ruling establishment believed the instrument had the power to incite rebellion. The bounty for informing to the authorities on Pipers was £5.00.

In Ireland in 1846 death from famine stalked the Irish landscape. The sound that was heard was not human, it was a guttural cry that seared the soul of the perpetrator, and filled the valleys of the Wicklow hills. In the distance there was a gathering, twenty five or more in a semi-circle in rags and in the throes of unspeakable sorrow. They were laying to rest two little boys aged 6 and 9 years who had just died of hunger. An uilleann piper was playing a haunting slow air at the graveside on an instrument that looked complicated and difficult to play. This was John Cash, The Piper. His pipes echoed the heartbreak of the women keening at the grave, and filled the air with a sorrow that could not be described in human terms.

All over the island of Ireland this scene was being repeated on a daily basis. Tens of thousands of men, women and children were

Top: John Cash
Bottom: John Cash's Will

16

being buried in mass graves, human beings eating grass like cattle to try and survive, and those who escaped this terrible hunger would eventually be taken down by an array of diseases. This was a tough, bitter environment where the chance of survival was practically nil. This was Ireland in 1846 - a dying race. In four years the population had fallen from 8.5 million people to less than 3 million.

John Cash was a tough individual, horse trader, Traveller, tinsmith and musician. He was an imposing figure, according to a colourful account provided by Capt James O'Neill in *Irish Minstrels and Musicians*:

> ***"For fancy, flashy shirts he had a strong weakness, while a broadcloth coat and a shining silk beaver hat completed his wardrobe and his happiness."***

He learned his survival instincts from a tough apprenticeship on the road with his father. He was one of a family of nine children. At night time he was to be found at the roadside campfire playing tunes on his uilleann pipes. Irish traditional music was being nurtured and kept alive in the most wretched conditions by John Cash, Traveller from Co Wicklow.
During his lifetime this giant of a man survived desperate conditions and amassed considerable wealth from his skills as a horse trader, and from his virtuosity on the uilleann pipes.

He had a real love of horses, and he travelled all over Ireland to horse fairs selling and buying horses, and playing Irish music for local isolated communities, as he camped at the roadside. He was a legendary figure at many major events in Ireland, and was easily recognisable because of his huge stature and musical ability.

John Cash had eight children and the eldest daughter Maggie, aged sixteen years, met and married another member of a Traveller family at a roadside funeral some years later. This man was called John Doran and he was also a knight of the road who could play Irish music on the uilleann pipes.
Their son, John Doran Jr, was also a piper. He married Kathleen

McCann from Rathnew in Wicklow, and they in turn had nine children; Ann, Ellen, Bridget, Maggie, Barbara, Patrick, Jim, Felix and Johnny.

The Eviction (Courtesy of Crawford Art Gallery Corp)

James Cash (1853 to 1890)

James Cash, often referred to as "Young Cash" in deference to his famous father, John, is believed to have been one of the most brilliant exponents of the pipes. His vast repertoire contained almost every music tune type-reels, single and double jigs, hornpipes, waltzes, marches and other music forms. He was highly regarded for his exquisite chanter work, and was in much demand at house dances, parties and weddings of the common man and nobility alike.

When he was nine years old, Young Cash went missing from the family home in Wexford, causing great anxiety to his parents. As his worried parents searched for him, they were attracted by a noisy crowd of juveniles on the main street. There they found young James with a miniature set of pipes, having completed a tour of the town, busking and carrying a large amount of silver and copper coins. The seeds of an illustrious career on the roads of Ireland playing music for a living had been sown.

While he was renowned for his exquisite chanter work, his use of the regulators was equally impressive. Many regarded him as a far superior piper to his father, and the famous Rowsome family, who had been central to sustaining the uilleann pipe tradition for more than five generations, was influenced by Young Cash. Samuel Rowsome, from Ballintore, Ferns, Co Wicklow was a well-known and versatile piper, and he was a regular visitor to the Cash household. Rowsome wrote to Captain Francis O'Neill(1848-1936), Chief of Police in Chicago, and a remarkable collector and publisher of Irish Traditional tunes. regularly informing him of the impact that Cash had on his own piping. The Rowsome family eventually settled in Dublin and began the long reign of a piping dynasty which has been so central to the survival of uilleann piping in the 20th and 21st centuries.

James Cash died a young man, unmarried, at the age of 37, and Ireland was deprived of "an effervescent genius".(O'Neill, F.1913)

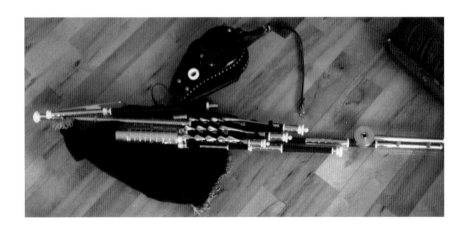

Left: James Cash (Courtesy of Bridget Cash)
Above: Dave Williams Pipes(Courtesy of Tommy Fegan)

Unknown Traveller family with ass and cart (Courtesy of Navan Travellers Workshops)

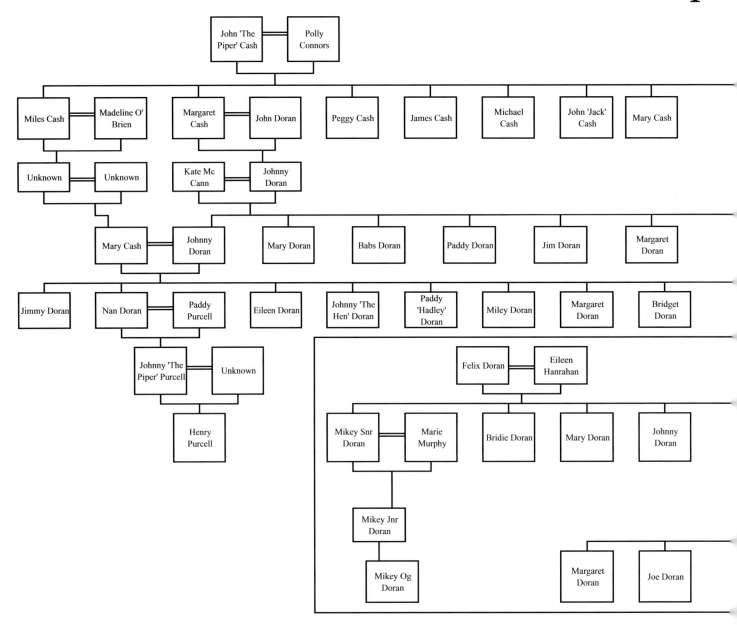

ynasty (Family Tree)

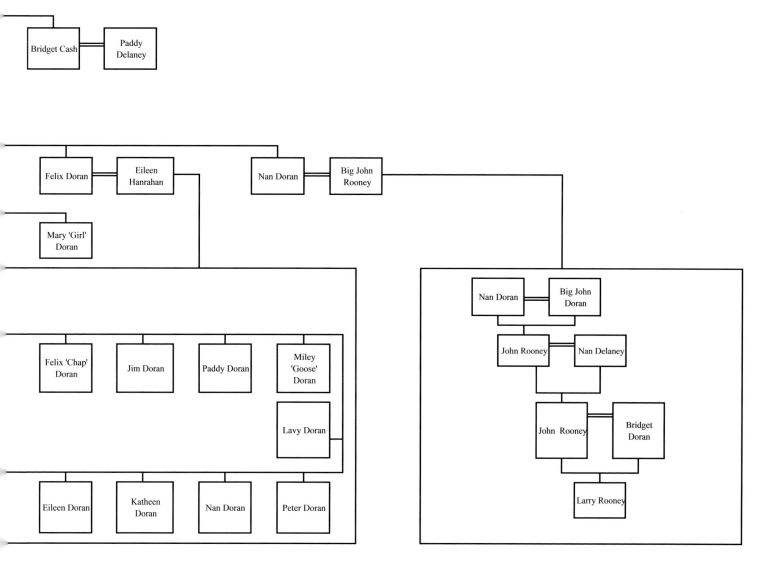

Chapter 2: Johnny Doran (1908-1950)

"You'd know that spring was here when you saw the crows building their nests, and when you saw the primroses growing at the side of the road, and when you saw Doran's caravan coming over the brow of the hill." George Callaghan, East Clare, 2006

As the 20th century unfolded, Ireland was recovering from the economic and cultural aftermath of a century of famine and turbulence, and post-famine Ireland was economically bankrupt, with very little money in circulation, no jobs, and food being rationed. The emerging Celtic revival saw the rise of the GAA, a resurgence of interest in the Irish language and a reawakening of pride in traditional music, giving momentum to political, economic and cultural upheavals that would transform Ireland in the new century ahead. Sadly, mass emigration continued to be the only solution for the survival of many. Families were broken up forever, death and disease was rampant and because of British rule and the inherent hardship perpetrated on the Irish race by the colonial power, unrest and rebellion was in the air. This was an unwelcoming place for those with political and cultural aspirations, and Irish Travellers were even more victimised than the local population.

Life must have been very hard for John Doran Sr and his wife Kate McCann at the turn of the century with their six children (they eventually had a family of nine children). The musical legacy had now been handed-down from his grandfather, the great John Cash, and John Doran was using this inherited skill to feed his family. Playing Irish music on the streets of Ireland was a Cash/Doran family tradition, and the next generation of Dorans were destined for the same lifestyle.

In January 1908, the Doran family and future generations of Irish musicians were blessed with the birth on the roadside of one Johnny Doran, who was to become one of the most influential Irish musicians in Irish folklore.

Johnny Doran was born in Rathnew, Co Wicklow in 1908. His parents, John Doran and Kate McCann, were both from a long line of Irish Travellers who played Irish music. Johnny learned a lot of piping from his father John, who was indebted to his grandfather, John Cash. (1832-1906). "Cash the Piper" as he was known, was widely regarded as the patriarch of the musical dynasty of the Cashs and Dorans. Cash's contribution to uilleann piping, and to the Irish Traveller tradition, is documented in Chapter 2 above.

Doran spent most of his short adult life travelling through most counties of Ireland and earning a living, mainly from playing uilleann pipes at fairs, races, football matches and other public events. He was very devoted to his family and to his Catholic faith. Two of his daughters, Nan and Eileen recall that he had just finished saying his prayers, and was tying his boot laces when a wall fell on top of his caravan on January 30th, 1948 near Christchurch in Dublin, where he was parked up for the winter. Doran was severely injured, and, despite being paralysed from the waist down, he continued travelling for over a year. The injuries he sustained from that accident led to his death in Athy in 1950.

Left: Johnny Doran with his pipes.

Above: Stock made and engraved by Johnny Doran, note how he spelt his name.
(Courtesy of Na Píobairí Uilleann)

Abuse of alcohol is a trait that has been attributed to many Irish Travellers and Irish traditional musicians. Against such stereotypical perceptions, Johnny Doran's abstinence from alcohol consumption further endeared him to the settled community. Doran was regarded by everyone, Traveller and non-Traveller alike, as honest, hardworking and very eager to help others, especially those wishing to acquire or learn to play uilleann pipes. That highly respected members of the settled community, such as Seán Reid, Assistant County Engineer with Clare County Council and Leader of the Tulla Céilí Band from 1947 until the mid-1960's, and others would organise benefit Céilís for Doran's family while he was dying, goes some way to indicate the esteem in which he was held.

Johnny Doran's musical travelling career spans the years of the early-1920s to the 1940s. This period corresponded with the early years of the new Irish Free State, the aftermath of the Civil War, the global depression of the 1930s and the economic consequences of World War II. Life was challenging for citizens of the new nation state, but it was even more so for those deemed to be second-class citizens. The hardships endured by Travellers, and the effects on infant mortality rates within their community, were never far from the daily lives of the young Doran family.

From a very early age John Doran Sr had introduced his son Johnny to the uilleann pipes, as he knew life on the road was going to be very hard, and he knew that young Johnny needed something extra to ensure he too would have a livelihood to support his family. Johnny was a natural born musician, and by the age of 8, he was proficient on this most difficult of instruments. He accompanied his father to horse fairs, race meetings and matches all over Ireland. They targeted any venue where crowds were guaranteed, and with his father John Sr busking on the street and collecting money, Johnny soon realized that this was a good way to make a living. He took the playing of the instrument very seriously, and in a short time became a very proficient piper.

John Doran's family eventually consisted of nine children, and music was to play a major part in providing for this family in this harsh environment. Johnny's brother Felix, who also adopted the pipes and became a great piper in his own right (see Chapter 4), was born during the Easter rebellion of 1916, when the sacrifices of the few

Johnny Doran , Aul Lamas Fair, Ballycastle. Circa 1930s

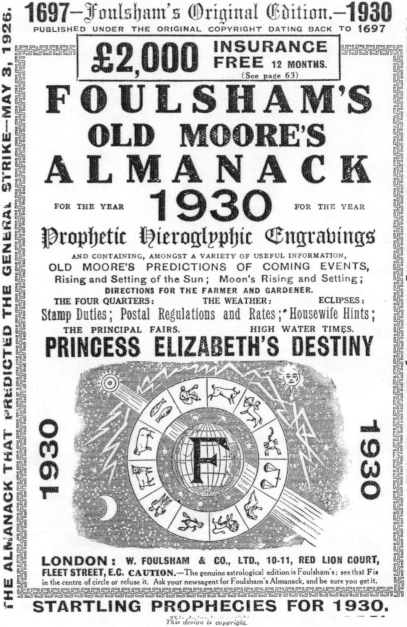

Old Moore's Almanack
Johnny Doran's travel guide
Circa 1930s(Courtesy of Co Clare Library)

would set in motion a chain of events that would lead to the War of Independence, the Civil War and the momentous events that would be the backdrop to the young Travellers' struggle for survival and acceptance.

John Doran was playing the pipes in Dublin city at the time of the Easter Rising in 1916, just as fellow piper Eamonn Ceannt was taking up arms with his colleagues.

This was Ireland now in another tough era. John Doran Sr took his children on the road. The horse drawn caravan was now the mode of transport and the entire island of Ireland from Wicklow to Donegal was the stage for the young Doran.

In the early summer of 1918, at just 10 years of age, young Johnny Doran accompanied his father to a horse fair in Carlow town, where there was a huge gathering of horse traders and onlookers. They both played their instruments on the corner of Tullow St, and within minutes, a large crowd had gathered to listen to the music of father and son on this strange but melodic instrument. Pennies, sixpences and old shillings were tossed into a collection box with abandon from an eager and appreciative audience. At day's end there was four pounds nine shillings and sixpence in the box. This was a substantial amount of money for a day's work, and it would feed the Doran family for at least four weeks.

Young Johnny Doran quickly realised the potential such a lifestyle could offer him after his first outdoor performance with the pipes, and decided this life of travelling the Irish roads and playing music for the masses was to be his future. Johnny decided that the Irish countryside should be the arena for his music, rather than just the locality near Wicklow where they lived, and he mapped his journey around Ireland, strategically targeting, fairs, race meetings, football matches and sports events. Johnny used *Old Moore's Almanac*, an old Irish publication that mapped all these events, as his route planner.

In 1922 old John Doran made his first appearance in Co Clare. He arrived in the village of Kilkishen in East Clare and parked his caravan on the nearby Kilgorey Road.

Kilkishen is a quiet peaceful little village in East Clare, nestled

Map Showing Johnny Doran's Travels (Courtesy of PJ O' Connell)

midway between Tulla and Sixmilebridge. Nothing much ever happened in this little hamlet, and it is strange that old John Doran picked this spot to park his caravan. At 2.30 pm, he called into the Black Stix Pub and Grocery shop and met a well-known man from the Broadford area of east Clare, Martin Rochford, who had an interest in the art of uilleann piping, having heard some recordings in the past.

Martin loved music and in conversation with old John Doran he discovered that John's son Johnny, who was then only 14 years old, was an excellent piper, and he promised Martin he would take young Johnny down to the pub that night. Just after half nine, the Dorans arrived in the Black Stick pub, and very soon an Irish music session was in full swing. Young Johnny sat on the outside of the crowd watching and listening to the older generation. After about an hour, Martin Rochford asked Johnny to play a few tunes. When he started to play the pipes, a hush fell on the crowd as everyone stood and gasped at the skill of the young performer.

The most defining feature of Johnny Doran's playing was the way in which his music embodied the wildness, the freedom of the open countryside, the flowing rivers, nature, the sounds of birds and other expressions associated with life on the road for a Traveller piper. It was raw, pure music from the depths of the soul of a man imbued with a rare talent.

Co Clare had been introduced to an exceptionally talented young uilleann piper, and Johnny was hooked on the appreciative audience he encountered. It was here, in this western county, that Johnny Doran made his special place of residence when he visited a number of times each year, for the rest of his life. Over a period of about twelve years young Johnny Doran made regular appearances in Co Clare, sometimes in East Clare near Broadford, sometimes in West Clare in Kilrush or Miltown Malbay, but wherever he appeared, there was a huge appreciative audience waiting, and soon the county was welcoming this bard with open arms.

Martin Talty, in his contribution to *A Famous Piper, a Long Note* production by RTÉ in 1988, recalled his first exposure to Johnny Doran and his music. In Miltown Malbay on a stormy afternoon, as Doran was playing *The Tarbolton Reel* in the doorway of a shop in Miltown; two very interested gentlemen were watching and listening. These were local musicians Martin Talty and his friend Willie Clancy, who were completely enthralled by the haunting sound of Doran's pipes.

When Johnny finished playing, Talty and Clancy accompanied him on his horse and cart to his caravan which was parked at the Old Forge near Quilty. There they sat and listened to him playing, enthralled with his virtuosity on this demanding instrument. Clancy was fascinated by the pipes and he got instruction from Johnny

Photo at St. Brigids Well, Liscannor of Johnie Doran (piper(taken in the 1930's when he travelled with his brother Felix to races, fair days, pattern days at Holy Wells etc. Sitting beside Johnie Doran is John Clair of Kineilty, Liscannor (Séan An Éithigh) storyteller and seanachaí, grandfather of Jimmy Carrucan, Fanore. Seated on the left is Mrs. Burke, caretaker of St. Brigids Well.

Above: Johnny Doran St Brigid's Well, Co Clare 1930s
Below: Johnny Doran advertised in the Clare Champion 1936. Playing for a harvest dance in West Clare. (Courtesy of Paul and Ollie Markham)

Doran on how to master them. When Doran came to Clare, Willie Clancy was his first visitor at the campsite, and they would play music in the caravan. Willie was accompanied on his visits by his friend Martin Talty, and they travelled with Doran to the races in Kilkee and Kilrush. At one of those famous outings Doran played the pipes, Clancy danced a hornpipe, and Talty collected the money for Doran.

Clancy himself very soon became an accomplished piper, and today the Willie Clancy week in Miltown Malbay is a testimony to Clancy, and by implication to the musical influence of Johnny Doran.

The Willie Clancy Summer School is organised every year by two great men, Muiris O'Rochain and Harry Hughes, both of whom are experts on the Traveller pipers of long ago. The School attracts thousands of pupils during the weeklong event, held during the first week of July, which celebrates the life and music of Willie Clancy. Classes in every traditional instrument, as well as set dancing, are provided by the very best performers possible, many of them, like James Kelly, returning from America each year to pass on the flame. Johnny Doran could never have foreseen the influence the young Clancy, who was so eager to learn the art of uilleann pipe playing from Doran, would have on generations of Irish traditional music enthusiasts from all over the world. The Doran legacy is alive and the flame is kept alight by Muiris O'Rochain and Harry Hughes.

John Kelly

John Kelly, father of James, the West Clare fiddle player, was awestruck by Johnny Doran, then just 24 years old, from the first time he saw him in Kilkee in Co Clare in 1932. He said he had never seen a musician like him and was mesmerized by Johnny's skill on the pipes and the way he would play them while standing one leg on a box in order to operate the chanter on his thigh. Johnny, John Kelly and Willie Clancy became great friends, and when Kelly moved to Dublin in 1944 and bought a shop in Capel St called the Horse Shoe, Doran would visit often. He loved the brown bread that Kelly's wife Frances baked for him(Frances was born in Co Wicklow, like Doran).

Times were tough in Dublin with World War II and its legacy, so Kelly's shop was open late at night and when it closed Doran and Kelly played tunes, drink tea and eat Frances Kelly's brown bread. One night in 1948, Johnny arrived and complained of chest pains to John Kelly. This was a major concern to Kelly and he advised Johnny to see a doctor. Kelly walked into the sitting room and said to his wife, "I think Johnny Doran is going to die" and he walked to the phone and contacted Kevin Danaher of the Irish Folklore Commission. Luckily Danaher was at home.

Kelly explained, "I have Johnny Doran here and I need him to be recorded," and Danaher replied without hesitation, "Bring him over straightaway".

Kevin Danaher later recalled how he saw this small man arriving with his pipes in a bag, and when the recording was set up, he began to play. Doran was mesmerized with the ball of acetate that was forming from the recording and he grabbed it and took it home "to show it to the missus".

These were the only recordings ever made of Johnny Doran, and the world of Irish traditional music owes a huge debt of gratitude to John Kelly for his vision in getting Doran recorded. Otherwise we would all have missed out on so much, as his 40 minutes of recording are iconic and unmatched from a piper of his calibre at that time in Ireland.

John Kelly, (Courtesy of John Kelly Jr.)

Left: Photo of John Doran (Father of Johnny Doran)
Above: Crowe's Bridge in Quilty, Johnny Doran's parking spot in West Clare

Doran's Music

Doran's music was fast and furious, but never out of control. His chanter playing laid down an endless stream of variations, remaining faithful to the basic melody line, yet exploring every opportunity to prevent the listener from any complacency that could arise from slavish repetition. Next, he made full use of the range of cord and note accompaniment which the three regulators provide. As with the chanter work, he moved freely between open (legato) and tight (staccato) fingering, and at times provides simultaneous deployment of both styles on the chanter and regulators. To heighten the dynamic tension that this endless range of options provides, Doran occasionally deployed the regulator keys to complete a melody line. A good example of this occurs in *The Blackbird* where, at the end of the first part, he holds the bottom D note on the chanter as he taps three D's on the baritone regulator. The same technique appears across many of his tunes including *The Sweeps* and *The Harvest Home* hornpipes, as well as in many of his reels. Doran did play for dancers, as well as playing to listening audiences at fairs, races and

28

Living in the bungalow beside the stone was an eighty year old man, George Chambers, who suddenly saw the activity and inquired from the workmen what was happening. They told him they were from the Council and they were widening the road and removing this big stone that was an obstruction. He told them that the stone could not be touched because in the 1930s Johnny Doran sat on that stone and played the pipes for the people of Clare, and he was not going to allow any Council to remove Johnny Doran's stone. After a major confrontation with the determined protester, the Council relented and the stone remains there to this day on a plinth, erected by the grateful people of the village, on the street.

That an eighty year old man was inspired to preserve a stone and persuade the Council to change the route of the road to commemorate the memory of a Traveller some 30 years after his death, gives us some indication of how revered Johnny Doran was in his adopted county. George Chambers died in 2009 aged 93 years.

In 1946 at the Spanish Point races, Johnny Doran collected £13-8-0 in one day's busking, at a time in Ireland when the annual wage for

football matches, and so the discipline of a steady rhythm is an integral part of his playing.

Johnny Doran was undoubtedly one of the most loved and respected musicians in the country in the 1930s and 1940s, and everywhere he went he was welcomed with open arms. He was invited into people's homes where he played for country dances. Michael Falsey from Quilty, where Doran often visited and camped, recalled another story of Doran's generosity. "There was a party in a house in Quilty, West Clare, in the late 40s, for a girl who was going to America. Her father sent his son on pony and trap for Johnny Doran who arrived with the pipes and played all night for the party. At the end of the night the man of the house put some money into Johnny's pocket and Johnny took it out and gave it back to his host, and said "No need to do that".

He and his family were given food, drink, money, accommodation, hay for his horses, and shelter for his caravan- anything they wanted. He was without question County Clare's adopted son and today the old people still recall with great affection the love and respect they had for this Traveller musician who brought so much joy into their hearts in a difficult period in Irish history.

In the picturesque village of Ballynacally, 13 kilometers outside Ennis, there is a large stone on the side of the road.In the late 1980s Clare County Council were widening the road on a narrow stretch at the bottom of the street. The workmen duly arrived with compressors, and trucks, and workmen with road signs to widen the road and remove the stone.

Above: Martin Rochford East Clare Fiddler and uilleann piper, close friend of Johnny Doran (Courtesy of Na Píobairí Uilleann)
Top Left: Johnny Doran Plaque in Ballynacally, Co Clare.

a farm laborer was £12-0-0 per year. This is testimony to the extent to which his music was appreciated, and it is unlikely any musician will ever achieve such a cult status in the modern Ireland of the 21st Century.

Johnny travelled the length and breadth of Ireland in a horse drawn caravan, and while most Travellers had a "Barrel Top" wagon, Johnny's was a "Flat Top". As Martin Rochford recalled, "A heavy ould thing that would test any horse", but of course it was instantly recognizable, instilling great anticipation and excitement at Doran's long-awaited return after a long, dreary winter. "They would know 'twas Doran a mile off" said Rochford.

Johnny would appear on many Saturday evenings in 1936 and 1937 in Eyre Square in Galway where he would entertain the masses. He was a fixture at this high profile venue, and it must have been something special to hear his pipes ringing out over Galway city. He would be on his way back from the Ballinrobe races and the mapped out journey would take him through Galway, on his way to Clare and Tipperary. Killenaule in Tipperary was another favorite haunt of Doran's where today he is still respected and loved.

Some of his travels around Ireland brought him to Counties Donegal and Sligo. He was playing the pipes in a laneway in Bundoran in the 1940s when Lad O'Byrne, the famous Sligo fiddler, on a visit back from the USA, heard him play. O'Byrne was from the Killoran/Coleman country around Gurteen in Sligo and of course Doran's piping caught his attention. He approached Doran and asked him to play *The High Level* hornpipe and, according to an eyewitness, Doran made a magnificent job of it. When he was finished playing O'Byrne gave him a half crown, a lot of money in those times, so pleased was he with Doran's rendition of the tune.

While Irish Travellers were marginalized in Irish society, Doran enjoyed unprecedented hospitality everywhere he went. In Kilfenora there was always a bed kept for Doran in Jim McCormack's house. Jim was a member of the famous Kilfenora Céilí Band of the 50s and 60s. Michael Falsey from Quilty recalls the first time he met Doran at the Spanish Point Races in West Clare in 1943.

"Doran came in behind me, he opened a case, put on the pipes and standing with one foot on the case, played away. He was a young man then with a black head of hair, and he had a peak cap and he gave the cap to his wife Mary, and she had a scarf around her head, gypsy type, and she would go round the crowd to collect for Johnny, holding out the cap saying "Assist the Musician". He was never without a collar and tie; they were not ordinary Travellers, and they were a cut above the other Travellers. The money flowed into that cap and people at the time did not have much" (Michael Falsey, 2009)

Eileen & Nan Doran

Johnny's daughters, Nan and Eileen, recalled for us how their father taught them to dance, and played for them as they rehearsed. It is not widely known that Johnny Doran was an exceptional dancer and regularly danced on his travels. Just like he did with his music, he told his daughters to do their best but "hold something back" so that there was an extra piece to give the audience later.

The full extent of Johnny's journey throughout Ireland is borne out by the fact that his children were born in Dublin, Down, Clare, Carlow, Sligo and Tyrone. Nan was born in Magherafelt Co Derry. Miley Doran was born in Daisy Hill Hospital, Newry Co Down. This is consistent with Nan's recollection of their dad busking on the passenger ferry between Warrenpoint and Omeath in Carlingford Lough.

Jimmy Doran

Jimmy Doran, Johnny's son, recalled his dad being arrested by the Gardai at the Monaghan/Armagh border. Butter and tea were being rationed and Doran had some hidden under the floorboards of his wagon. He was released when a Garda recognized him as Johnny Doran the piper and he persuaded the sergeant to let him go, but he had to play for them and when he did, the sergeant released him without charge.

Irish Travellers like Doran were skilled men who could improvise on the road. Doran would use the steel rim of the wagon as an anvil and

Above: Eileen and Nan Doran, daughters of Johnny Doran and wonderful sources of information on Johnny Doran's life.

made regulator keys out of spoons. He had an ingenious solution for every problem, as can be appreciated by a story recounted by Tommy Sands, the folk singer from Co Down, recalling Doran's ingenuity in uilleann pipe maintenance. Sands remembers Jack Makem, brother of the famous folk singer, Tommy Makem, talking about Doran's visit to Armagh. Jack had his first set of pipes and they had developed a leak. Doran examined them and asked him if he had a hot water bottle. He cut a hole in the side of the bottle for the connection to the bellows and adapted the neck to house the chanter. This enabled Makem to continue playing the pipes.

When Johnny Doran told John Kelly in 1948 that he had chest pains, Kelly's instincts to get him recorded immediately proved to be a masterstroke as faith dealt a cruel blow to this great man some months later. His caravan was parked in High Street in Dublin, and he was bent down tying his shoe laces, when the storm blew the wall beside the caravan in on top of the wagon. He was surrounded by his children and miraculously none of them were hurt. Eileen and Nan (Purcell) his daughters recall the accident and the impact it had on their family. It was utter devastation and they remember their Dad lying on the ground covered in rubble. The stone crushed the caravan and broke his back. He was severely injured and the Irish Press at the time reported the incident. We were presented by Nan with a photograph of Johnny Doran on the ground covered with a blanket, minutes after the accident. This picture was taken by an amateur photographer, who happened to be there when the accident occurred. It was given to Johnny's wife, Mary, after his death, and their daughter, Nan, had kept it with her in England ever since. She asked that it be included in the book, as it has never been seen by anyone outside the immediate family until now.

Even though he lived for two years after the accident, Doran never again played the pipes except when Willie Clancy, Andy Conroy and Seán Reid went to see him in hospital. They fixed the bag and bellows on him and Clancy operated the bag and Doran played the chanter. Johnny Doran died at age 42 on the 19th January, 1950 in Athy and is buried close to his brother Felix in the Rathnew, Co. Wicklow cemetery. Ireland, and the world of Irish music lost a legend on that fateful morning.

It was raining on Thursday morning 21st January 1950. In a grey,

bleak building on the north side of Dublin there was a roll call and 50 or 60 young boys lined up in the hallway of a cold, unplastered building that had an aura of misery and hardship. One little boy was only 12 years old and he was looking at the clock on the wall. The time was almost 12 o'clock and this little boy knew that something major was happening in Dublin and he was not allowed to be there. This little boy was Jimmy Doran and he is the son of Johnny Doran, who was being buried after the accident in his caravan two years earlier. In those times when one parent died, the local authority took some of the children into care and they became part of a strict regime where discipline played a major part in their young lives.

It was 60 years later that Jimmy recalled his disappointment at not being allowed to attend his dad's funeral and be with his mum on this sad day. Tough times, in a tough unforgiving Irish environment.

Jimmy can recall with accuracy his father's visits all over Ireland but to Clare in particular. Jimmy proudly boasts, "I was born in Clare, I am a Clare man", but he could not remember where in Clare he was born. During our research for this publication we discovered that Mary Doran, Jimmy's mum, was admitted to St. Joseph's Hospital

Above: Jimmy Doran son of Johnny Doran
Below: Johnny The Hen Doran, son of Johnny Doran at the Wicklow Doran Tiónol (2000) (Courtesy of Alphie Mulligan)

Above: Johnny Doran in the rubble of the collapsed wall and caravan, Dublin, 1948. (Courtesy of Nan Doran)

in Ennis on the 6th July 1936 where young James was born and they were both discharged on the 13th July 1936. According to Johnny's daughters, Nan and Eileen, their father had been saving his money with the intention of buying a farm in Co Clare, coming off the road and raising his young family amongst the people who had adopted him and his music. He was anxious that they received a proper education, and that they would be accepted in the local community. He told them he could think of no better place in Ireland to settle down than Co Clare.

Doran was without question a genius, a master musician and a true gentleman, loved and respected by all who came in contact with him. He was welcomed into their homes, was given food to eat, feed for his horses, and he was invited to their weddings. He was given whatever money they had, when he played the pipes for them. He was a truly remarkable individual who entertained communities all over Ireland, in an austere and challenging times for the fledgling nation..

The legacy of Doran is now forever enshrined in the annals of uilleann piping and a testimony to his genius can be found every year at the Doran Tionól, in Spanish Point, Co Clare where uilleann pipers-Travellers and non-Travellers alike, from the four corners of the globe assemble to honor the tradition and genius of Johnny Doran, Traveller, musician, and protector of our tradition.

Johnny Doran gravestone in Wicklow (Courtesy of Leo Rickard)

Musicians influenced by Johnny Doran

The impact of Johnny Doran and his playing can be gauged on two levels;
1.   Those who met Doran and experienced his playing first-hand, and
2.   Countless pipers who were influenced by the 12 tracks of music recorded in 1948 by the Irish Folklore Commission.
A small sample of some of the better known musicians influenced by Doran includes the following;

Finbar Furey

Finbar Furey is probably one of the best know Irish Traveller traditional musicians and undoubtedly was to the fore in introducing the sound of the uilleann pipes to the burgeoning audience for Irish folk and traditional music, at home and abroad, from the early 1960's. Finbar's first memories, aged about six, of Johnny Doran was hearing a tape of his which his father Ted had, and he was able to slow it down for Finbar.

"My father would just say, "listen to what he is playing, and I listened to what he was playing, and I listened to the style of his fingers. And it was beautiful and I learnt from listening to Johnny".
(Furey, F. Spawell Hotel, Dublin Friday 31, July 2009)

Ted was friendly with both Johnny and Felix and, according to Finbar, the brothers would argue over who was going to busk with Ted.

"Cause the auld fella had the banjo and of course all pipers like to play with the banjo because it gives it a good lift; it's a good combination, and of course when you're busking the loudness always wins. The loudest instrument will always win".

Musical Traveller families, like the Dorans, the Fureys, the Dunnes and the Keenans, would keep in touch with one another when they were on the road. When Johnny Doran was in Co Clare, and when Ted Furey and his family were travelling through Galway, they would arrange to meet and exchange tunes that they had picked up. Similarly, the Dorans and the Dunnes, Traveller musicians from Limerick, adopted the same routine. The Dorans often called at the Dunnes encampment, requesting a fiddler to accompany them in their busking for the day. They also exchanged information about locations where they would get a good reception.

Finbar's final word on Doran; "Johnny Doran, he was probably the greatest player I ever heard in my life."

Mickey Dunne

Mickey Dunne has inherited much of the Traveller piping and fiddling traditions from his father, Paddy and his uncles, Mick, Hanta, and Christy, known collectively as the Blind Dunne Brothers. They achieved celebrity status as Traveller musicians in counties Limerick, Cork, Kerry, Tipperary and Clare in the 30's and 40's.(See Chapter 5), and two of them featured on Gay Byrne's *Late, Late Show* in the early 1900's. Mickey is a highly respected piper and fiddler, and has produced some fine CD's accompanied by his two daughter's Niamh and Bríd. Mickey talks about Johnny Doran's self-sufficiency, claiming that he could make his own caravan, pipes, reeds, regulator keys etc. "My father (Paddy Dunne) made his own caravan and also Ted Furey and Johnny Doran, they were all the same gifted men who could make anything."

(Postcolonial Artist, *Johnny Doran and Irish Travellers Tradition*, Touhy, D. and O'hAodha, M. (2008), Cambridge Scholars Publishing, Newcastle, p79)

Mickey Dunne continues to promote uilleann pipe playing, and especially the style of Irish Travellers. He makes and repairs pipes, and is in great demand for lectures and performances throughout Ireland and abroad. Mickey is one of the most eloquent and enthusiastic advocates of the piping styles of Johnny and Felix Doran, relentlessly committed to ensuring their music is never forgotten.

Paddy Keenan

Paddy Keenan's piping was pivotal to the sound of the Bothy Band, which played a key part in the revival of Irish traditional music in the early 1970s. Keenan's piping faithfully evokes the Traveller style of piping characterized mainly by Johnny Doran. Keenan stated that Doran was special. His control and his mastery of the instrument were phenomenal. He said that Johnny Doran was the single biggest influence in his playing. He could produce spectacular music on the uilleann pipes. Paddy also stated that Doran's piping reflected the Ireland of the times and it is now so wonderful to see all the young modern pipers who want to play like Paddy Keenan, a style directly influenced by Johnny Doran and his music.

Willie Clancy (1918-1973)

The Willie Clancy Summer School is the biggest non-competitive gathering of Irish traditional musicians in Ireland. Primarily established to celebrate the uilleann piping of Willie Clancy, it caters for thousands of students learning traditional music in almost every instrument during the first week of July. Willie Clancy fell under the spell of Johnny Doran at an early age. Martin Talty was with Willie when he first saw the pipes being played by Johnny Doran at the races in Milltown Malbay in 1936. "Straight away a friendship was struck up between boy and man that culminated in Johnny becoming his first teacher - and what an apt pupil Willie turned out to be." (Talty, M. *Treoir*, 1973. Comhaltas Ceoltóirí Éireann, Dublin.)

The young Clancy was clearly in awe of Doran, and he used to cycle from Miltown Malbay to Quilty a journey of six kilometers,

and other locations in West Clare to hear Doran playing. Johnny's son, Jimmy, remembers the young Willie Clancy coming to their caravan in Clare, and following them around on a bike. On another occasion, according to Terry Wilson, Clancy cycled to Newcastle West in County Limerick (approximately 70 miles) when he heard through the grapevine that Doran was in Newcastle West busking on the street.

Although he got his first set of pipes from Felix Doran, it is Johnny's music that is clearly in evidence in the playing of Willie Clancy. And its Clancy's music that has attracted tens of thousands of devotees to the annual Willie Clancy Summer School each year for the last 40 years.

Muiris O'Rochain and Harry Hughes, organisers of the Annual Willie Clancy Summer School in Co. Clare. (Courtesy of Tony Kearns) The sad news of Muiris' passing reached us just as we were going to print. We had hoped that he could have seen the book, but that was not to be. Irish music has lost a great champion.

Martin Rochford (1916-2000)

Martin Rochford was another Co. Clare musician on whom Johnny Doran made a powerful impression. While Martin had initially been lured to the uilleann pipes after hearing another Traveller, Tony Rainey, playing pipes in Ennis in the 1930s, it was Doran who encouraged him to get his own set of practice pipes.

Johnny Doran told Rochford of a practice set worth buying. He sold them to Dan McMahon in Ennis. So in 1936 Martin got his first practice set for £2-0-0 from McMahon of Parnell St., Ennis. Although Rochford, who was versatile on fiddle and pipes, was influenced by fiddlers, his repertoire was speckled with tunes closely associated with the Dorans. These included the *Morning Star*, the two *Copperplates, the Steampacket, Rakish Paddy, the Swallow's Tail, My Love is in America* and others. Martin's greatest source of pride was the notation for Doran's own version of the *Swallow's Tail*, which Doran wrote out for him in 1938. (Laban, P. *An Pobaire*, Volume 4 Issue 1, Na Píobairí Uilleann , Dublin)

Martin Talty (1920-1983)

Martin Talty, a highly regarded piper from Co Clare, was fascinated by Doran's dexterity on the chanter. He noted that "He had a peculiar thing, you know, all his fingers seem to be the same length. You got the impression that this finger was warbling around the chanter. He was probably what they call double jointed."
In his interview with Robert van Dijk, in Milltown Malbay in 1979, Talty explained some of the techniques which distinguished Doran's playing.

"In *Rakish Paddy* he used to play the C natural, and then he stopped the chanter, and played this regulator accompaniment. I don't know if it is in his recordings, but he used to do it that way.

Switching the drones off and on, during a tune, was a trick of the old pipers. And in the airs, they topped off two drones and they let the tenor go".
(Van Dijk, R.(1995) *An Píobaire*, Volume 4 Issue 10)

Seán Reid (1907-1978)

Seán Reid was a county engineer with Clare County Council for many years, but he was better known for his commitment to uilleann pipe playing. Seán played with many of the greatest traditional musicians at one time or another, including Joe Cooley, Paddy Canny, P.J. Hayes, Peter O'Loughlin, Bobby Casey, Martin Talty, Martin Rochford and Willie Clancy. He was also the leader of the Tulla Céilí Band from the mid-40s to the mid-60s, and he was renowned for his generosity and kindness.

A good example of this was demonstrated at the time when Doran's health was rapidly deteriorating in the hospital in Athy. Doran lay on his deathbed, Sean organized a benefit Céilí at Quilty Co. Clare for Johnny and his family. The Seán Reid Society, founded in honor of this generous patron of the pipes, publishes a periodical dedicated to piping, and a central theme of the publications is the high regard in which Doran and his music is hailed universally.

Sgt Armstrong

Tom Armstrong was a Garda Sgt, stationed in Newbridge, Co Kildare in the 1930s. He played uilleann pipes in the Rowsome style, making copious use of the regulators. While stationed there, he befriended Liam Flynn, father of Liam Óg O'Floinn, one of the most celebrated uilleann pipers today, and Liam Óg reflects with pride on the fact that Doran called to house when he was just a baby;

"I have no memory of it because I was a baby, but, apparently, Johnny Doran called to the house where I was born and reared in Kill. He called to Tom Armstrong in Newbridge. Tom said to him," When you're travelling onto Dublin, call into this man in Kill, he's a fiddle player." So he did. I was in the cradle when Doran came in and played a few tunes. One of the tunes, my father tells me, was a popular reel at the time, *The Sligo Maid*. It's certainly nice to know that Doran passed through."

(O'Toole, L. (2006) *The Humours of Planxty*, pps 21,24   Hodden Headline, Dublin)

The Legacy and the Legend

Johnny Doran's musical legacy is far reaching and fully appreciated by those who recognized his genius and the influence he brought to bear, directly and indirectly on the development of Irish traditional music in the second half of the 20th century. We have seen from a small sample of well known players (above) who acknowledge his influence on their playing, that his short playing career had a profound effect on them directly, and through them, an incalculable impact on subsequent generations of Irish traditional musicians. Musicians like Finbar Furey and Paddy Keenan became role models for aspiring young pipers since the early 60's. Their music, by their own admission, is shaped and styled on Doran's techniques. The Furey Brothers and Davy Arthur, as well as the Bothy Band, used the Doran sound to build a fresh, driving, attacking sense of wild abandon that would excite young followers across the world. In turn, new generations of non-Traveller pipers like Davey Spillane, and Michael "Blackie" O'Connell adopted the Doran sound and continue to bring it to new audiences, in their own recordings and performances, and as lead players in Riverdance, Lord of the Dance and other globetrotting shows.

Doran's limited recording material was broadcast briefly after it had first been recorded. While it took over 20 years to make the recording commercially available, some musicians were able to make copies of the original broadcast and well-known fiddle players and concertina players listened intently to Doran's interpretation of popular tunes.

At the Johnny Doran piping Tionól in Wicklow in 2004, Jimmy Doran gazes admiringly at the priests vestments made specially for the Doran Family by his daughters, Bridgie and Maggie Doran, depicting Johnny Doran's life and times.

The Piper Sleeps beneath the shrouds of Winter
His travelling way of life now almost gone,
His pipes of peace are resting, journey's over
His legacy of music living on
Cold death has kissed, the piper's breath was frozen
On dreams of yesterday's cruel ice crawls
The purest tones supreme to piping mysteries
Held tight now in the grip of nature's claws

No more he'll stray the lanes from Clare to Dublin
No more he'll pipe the fairs of rural towns
Or sit the milestone, tuning pipes for Clancy
His travelling style of music far beyond
Green tented wattles are no match for Winter
Would muggy straw warm a roadside bed?
Sweet sweet the pipes, and the hand and the heart that willed them
From a travelling man with no equal must be said

(Written by Finbar Furey in memory of Johnny Doran)

Chapter 3: Felix Doran (1916-1972)

The Man, His Music and His Family.

Johnny Doran passed away in 1950, and the family baton of entertaining the Irish public was now passed to his younger brother, Felix, a popular and charismatic figure who achieved cult status as an uilleann piper and entertainer.

This was a time when Irish Travellers were abandoning the horse-drawn wagon as their primary means of travelling. Although Felix continued travelling and playing his music throughout Ireland until 1952, the era of the slow-moving, horse-drawn wagon, as the primary means of transport for Irish Travellers, was drawing to an abrupt close.

Developments in technology and communications in the early 1950s heralded fundamental changes for the life-style of Irish Travellers. Cars and vans replaced the horse-drawn wagons, and the availability of low-cost plastic goods, such as buckets, rendered tinsmiths redundant, who traditionally repaired old and damaged tin household utensils. The increased availability of televisions and telephones obviated the dependency of isolated rural communities on Travellers to bring news from the outside word. While we can only speculate as to how Johnny Doran would have adapted to these sudden changes, his younger brother Felix coped well, developing business interests (dealing mainly in horses and feathers) in Ireland which complimented his continued travelling and music making.

One of the signatories to the Irish Proclamation, which was published in Dublin's GPO in 1916 on Easter Monday, was Éamonn Ceannt, an uilleann piper of note who was one of the founder members and secretary of the Pipers' Club in Thomas Street, Dublin. This building was later named Áras Ceannt after this illustrious, historical figure. Ceannt the piper possibly would have played pipes with old John Doran and John Cash

Eileen, Mikey and Felix Doran, Keele Folk Festival, 1966
(Courtesy of Brian Shuel)

Éamonn Ceannt 1916 proclamation signator and uilleann piper.

Sackville Street, (now O'Connell Street) Dublin, after the 1916 Easter Rising.

It was a remarkable coincidence that as this iconic figure, who featured so prominently in music and in the fight for Irish freedom, was executed in Kilmainham Gaol in April 1916, just as another legendary musical icon was about to enter the world. Felix Doran the piper was born two months later to Mary and John Doran, on 21st June, 1916 when the smell of cordite still hung in the Dublin air in the aftermath of the Irish Rebellion. Felix Doran's arrival was probably welcomed by the strains of the pipes now being taken up by his 8 year old brother Johnny. In 1908 Ceannt was a member of a party of Irish athletes who travelled to Rome for the Jubilee celebrations, and he had the honor of playing the pipes for Pope Pius X.

In 1922 at the end of another turbulent year of civil war in Ireland, Johnny Doran was a proficient uilleann piper and had just taken second place in the Oireachtas competition to Leo Rowsome. Felix was anxious to learn this instrument, and under Johnny's tutelage this eight-year-old was already showing signs of promise and genius on the uilleann pipes.

The Doran Clan was now on the road travelling all over Ireland and music was the daily diet of the family. It must have been wonderful to have experienced the campfire sessions at night time with this incredible musical family. As Mickey Dunne the Limerick piper once said, "I'd love to have been there". Mickey was also talking about his dad, Paddy Dunne, and his uncles who accompanied the Dorans on their travels and he maintained they played their best music at the campfire after busking.

Having travelled extensively throughout Ireland for more than three decades, Felix moved to Manchester where he established a very successful business. His eldest son, Mikey, still lives in Manchester, and although Mikey Sr was a very promising young piper who played for many years in his early teens with his father, he gave up the music to pursue his business interests, which, like his father's, were very successful.

My dad was always a dealer. Even if he had a drink or didn't have a drink, he had a good head for business. He dealt in horses and feathers. He didn't deal in furniture, perhaps a little bit in antiques. He dealt in non-ferrous metals. That was a big rage at the time. (Doran, M. Manchester 2009)

Micky Doran Sr, playing at the Doran Tionól. Co Clare, 2010.
(Courtesy of Leo Rickard)

Mikey hasn't played the pipes in over 40 years, yet he demonstrated, during the session of music which followed these interviews in 2009, that he was still able to produce fascinating tight fingering, steady rhythm and subtle harmonies on the regulators on pipes borrowed from the author.

Even though he worked diligently to establish his business, Felix Doran ensured that he maintained his musical interests. Each week he was to be found at one of the many sessions that were popular in Manchester at that time. He also availed of every opportunity to return to Ireland and link up with old friends who were musicians. Funerals, and other family occasions, often provided the chance to spend a few days back in Ireland and to keep in touch with fellow musicians. Unlike his brother Johnny, Felix enjoyed a drink, sometimes to excess, but never to the extent that it distracted from his family, business or musical interests. Above all else, according to his son Mikey, Felix was first and foremost a family man. Even to the extent that when Topic Records invited Felix to go on tour in America, he refused, simply because his wife didn't want him to go.

As a young man Felix took to the road, at the outset with brother Johnny, from whom he learned the fundamentals of the uilleann pipes, as well as the tricks of the trade of busking and earning a living from music. Initially, Felix was unsuccessful in persuading his older brother to teach him how to play the pipes. However, even at an early age, Felix's business instincts prevailed when he persuaded Johnny to give him lessons in exchange for Felix's bicycle, which Johnny had been eyeing with envy. Having acquired the fundamentals of piping from Johnny, Felix took the bike back. When Johnny protested, Felix invited him to take the lessons back! Eventually, Felix and Johnny travelled separately. Both of them were very popular in County Clare, where Felix concentrated on the eastern part of the county, while Johnny largely confined his playing to west Clare.

For most of his adult life, Felix played a silver set of pipes which he commissioned from a German engineer, Frank Gorker . Those pipes were on display at the 2010 Doran Tionól in Spanish Point, Co. Clare. Pipe maker Dave Williams' pipes are much in favor by Travellers; Paddy Keenan, John Rooney, Johnny Purcell and Mikey

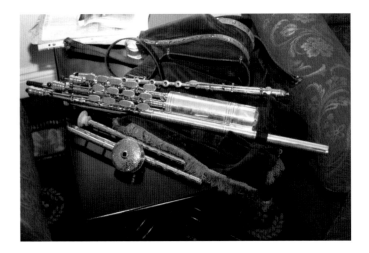

Above: Felix Doran's specially commissioned silver set of uilleann pipes (Courtesy of Leo Rickard. Co Clare, 2010)

Left: Mikey Doran Sr and Mikey Doran Jr, son and grandson of Felix Doran (Courtesy of Leo Rickard. Co Clare, 2010)

Doran Jnr are just a few who are proud owners of Williams' sets. Dave was an engineer by trade, and he took a lively interest in Felix's silver set. After much research, he concluded;

"Inspection showed that the pipes were made to a highly professional standard using techniques more similar to a brass instrument maker then a woodwind maker. The chanter and regulators were made from brass spun over a mandrill off the exact bore size. The tone holes and key mounts were then soldered onto the tube in the same way as a metal flute. The open holes of the chanter were fitted with flat finger plates to give the same feeling as a woodwind chanter. (Dave Williams was tragically killed in a car accident in 2005) After some research of makers in the Manchester area, I discovered that a German called Gorker had worked at Barratt's brass instrument makers in the 1950s and had later started his own electro plating business, it seems quite probable that this man made the pipes."

Brendan Breathanach confirmed that the pipes were very expensive as he recalls Felix remarking to him, "even the missus doesn't know how much they cost." (Williams, D. Manchester, 1985)

The Legacy and the Legend

Four years after Felix's death, Topic Records released the only commercial recording made by him, *The Last of the Travelling Pipers*. Seán Reid, the well-known Co. Clare piper and friend of Felix, contributed the sleeve notes to that recording. They provide a unique insight into Felix Doran, the musician as well as giving us a sense of Felix's personality, and therefore merit extensive referencing here;

"They (Felix and his brother Johnny) were the last of a great and illustrious line of travelling pipers, and the end of an era; it is unlikely that we shall ever see their likes again… I lived in Dublin for a year in 1934-35 and followed Felix around Moore Street enchanted by his piping. I recall him vividly as he was then - a handsome, well-built young fellow of 18 or 20 in a blue, double-breasted suit, very clean and tidy and wearing in his coat lapel the badge of the Pioneer Total Abstinence Association. I was living in Ennis, County Clare when in the course of his journeying around Ireland he turned up there in 1938. I had now pipes of my own and Felix was a frequent and welcome visitor at my home.

Felix Doran playing to an admiring public in Mullingar, 1963.

Living in a comfortable horse drawn caravan with his pretty young wife and a few small children he plied his business of horse-dealing and general trading while playing the pipes at fairs, markets and country dances all over the country. He was a pleasant-mannered, cheery young man who talked freely about himself and his life and adventures. He was gifted with a vivid imagination and never thought it any harm to improve a good story! I was able to supply him with a few good Rowsome chanter reeds from time to time.

He moved on again after a few months and the next time we met was at the Galway Races in 1944. He looked bronzed, relaxed and happy when, surrounded by an appreciative and generous audience; he filled sun-lit Eyre Square with the thrilling sound of his pipes. He returned again to Clare for the last time in the late autumn of 1950 and this time he had a large, white Austin van and was collecting old car-batteries and also old feather mattresses (ticks) which, he explained, were to be used in the manufacture of pound notes. He always had a good head for business and habitually kept a 50 pound note in his pocket. By this time he was coming up in the world and beginning to fill out and put on a little weight while his handsome leonine head and face was becoming more and more reminiscent of his famous great-grandfather, John Cash. Unfortunately, he had also become an alcoholic and was going on periodic bouts of heavy drinking which had a disastrous effect on his normally pleasant temperament. On one memorable occasion we (the Tulla Céilí Band, with Joe Cooley) brought him along to a dance at Kilkee where he brought the house down with *The Fox Chase*. After a few weeks he moved on again. The next time I saw him he was in his coffin.

In 1963 Felix won first prize on the pipes at Fleadh Cheoil na

hÉireann in Mullingar. Subsequently he settled down in Manchester where he became a wealthy haulage contractor with a great fleet of lorries. He engaged a skilled German mechanic to fashion him an all-silver set of pipes, a marvel of craftsmanship that must have cost a small fortune. In the middle 60's he was recorded and broadcast repeatedly on television and radio.

He died in 1972 in Manchester after a long illness and his funeral cortege from Dublin to Wicklow was the largest I ever saw, with the possible exception of Leo Rowsome's and Willie Clancy's . He was buried in Rathnew graveyard, some distance from Johnny. Two pipers, one of them his son, Michael, the other Neillidh Mulligan, played at his graveside. I estimated the pile of wreaths as being 9 feet long, 6 feet wide and 4 feet high. He was present at the last Fleadh Ceoil na hÉireann before his death.

If tributes count for anything then Felix died the uncrowned king of the travelling people. During his too short lifetime he gave a tremendous lift to Irish music, and especially to the uilleann pipes. He had something unique to contribute and is assured of a permanent and honourable place in the annals of Irish minstrels and musicians. Ar dheis Dé go raibh a anam (May his soul be at God's right hand)."

(Seán Reid, 1976) *The Last of the Travelling Pipers*, Felix Doran. Topic: 12T288.1976

As you walked up the main street you could hear the music. It filled the Monaghan air and ripples of excitement spread from the source of this music like rays from a sunset over Galway Bay in August, 1950. The crowd was bunched together at the street corner witnessing something exciting. The masses at the Fleadh Cheoil in this balmy August afternoon in Clones were being treated to a musical spectacle. He was sitting on a shop window sill, surrounded by an adoring public with his uilleann pipes strapped on and the music he was playing was spectacular, notes falling out of the chanter like droplets of winter sleet on a glass roof. Felix Doran, in full flight, was carrying

Previous page, The Doran Family
(Courtesy of Leo Rickard. Co Clare, 2010)

on a proud tradition that was eerily reminiscent of his older brother Johnny, who had passed to his eternal reward a few months earlier.

Felix was an Irish music legend who had travelled the lanes and byways of Ireland bringing his music to an adoring public. He was clearly at home in this environment, this window sill in Clones was his Carnegie Hall stage, and Doran was in full flight.

One elderly man on the perimeter of the street audience shook his head and said, "Jesus this is something". Doran was demonstrating his incredible prowess on the pipes to his adoring audience. In 1950s Ireland, Felix Doran was king of the uilleann piping fraternity.

From his time on the road, and from watching his brother Johnny perform in the open air, Felix knew how to work the crowd into frenzy. His genius on the pipes was complimented by a pleasing personality and exceptionally handsome features. Women adored him and men jostled to be in his company. He was also very generous of spirit and his kindness and generosity particularly to young and not so young pipers, was legendary.

It is well known that when Felix Doran entered a pub his presence filled the room and the crowds followed to hear him play. Landlords of pubs in Manchester that were haunts of Felix in the heady 60s and 70s spoke of him with reverence, and in counties all over Ireland, you can still hear tales of Felix Doran and his charisma.

Felix and Johnny Doran were music legends all over Ireland but it was in Clare that they seemed to have had their biggest impact. While Johnny seemed to have escaped any prejudices towards the Traveller community, nevertheless Felix did encounter some anti-Traveller sentiment.

Rory Kieran, a retired schoolteacher from Crossmaglen Co Armagh developed a close relationship with Felix and when Felix was back in Ireland, he would visit Johnny Rooney (father of John Rooney, Felix's son-in-law and an accomplished piper in the Doran tradition). Kieran recalls being regularly sent for to help Felix gain entry to public houses in Crossmaglen when he visited. Even though Felix would play and entertain the locals in pubs for many hours, thereby increasing the publican's income, he would not be admitted unless

he was chaperoned by Kieran.
(Kieran, R. Newry, 2010)

In Clare no such prejudices existed and the Dorans were welcomed everywhere. Felix concentrated in East Clare- Broadford, Scarriff, and Tulla-while Johnny concentrated on west Clare-Milltown, Kilrush, Kilkee and Ballynacally.

Michael Falsey, the Quilty piper, emphasizes the popularity of the Doran brothers in Co Clare;
"The country house dances were in full swing in those times and the Dorans were always in demand for the set dances. Although there were many local musicians around the area, the Dorans were a big boost to the events. A collection would be made at the door and a pound given to the piper. It was years after I took part in those dances and the Dorans had moved on, but they are still spoken of whenever there is a dance or a session. Most of their tunes were played for years after they left as the travelling musician was a great help to the local player for learning tunes."

Felix's Music

Felix's style of playing was different to Johnny's, as it was more measured and structured, and by all accounts more suitable to dancers. Both brothers were able to move freely between the open and closed styles. The open style suited the conditions under which Travellers performed. It produced more volume, which was critical when competing with the noise of the crowds at fairs and football matches. Felix's lifestyle differed from Johnny's as he adopted a largely "settled" lifestyle less dependent on music for an income and developed a performance style better suited to indoor session type conditions.

Felix's regulator playing is more reminiscent of Leo Rowsome's steady tapping, occasionally interspersed with a long note. Johnny's endless variations on the regulators are far removed from the Wexford style of constant vamping, exemplified by the Rowsomes, and Felix Doran.
During their lifetimes Felix and Séamus Ennis were respected pipers and their fame continues to this day. Felix was an open style player

whereas Séamus leaned more towards the closed style. Felix can, however, be heard making extensive use of tight fingering in the second part of the Lark in the Morning.

In spite of his undoubted talents and popularity, Felix Doran, like his brother Johnny, was neither boastful, arrogant nor aloof. He was generous in helping people acquire sets of pipes, giving instructions, helping with their maintenance and he was of course so generous with his music. His impact on the world of uilleann piping is huge and the rare footage of him playing the pipes in Mullingar with his son Mikey, is invaluable archival footage, and clearly shows his son Mikey in full unison with the master.

Mikey recalled his father's effective, if unusual, teaching technique;
"He used to ask me to go upstairs when he was learning me a few notes. He would sit in the chair below and would say "I can hear you." He had a high wire rigging and he wound it up through the wall and he'd say, "Go back, its wrong." Obviously he wanted the best out of me. My father could never read music and I couldn't either. Sometimes when I was playing I would lift the wrong finger, and he had a stick, "Not that one." (Mikey demonstrated how Felix would tap the offending finger; firmly enough to ensure the same mistake was not repeated.)
Paddy O'Donoghue, a well-known musician from East Clare recalled how Felix and his wife would arrive in Broadford in a horse drawn caravan in the 1940s/1950s and the welcome in East Clare for this musical troubadour was legendary.

There was a special place allocated in the O'Donoghue household for Felix's horses; there was firewood and turf for his fires, food for his family and a welcome for everyone. He would stay for up to three weeks at a time and the sessions were legendary. When it was time for him to depart, they would hide his horses so that he would stay a little longer with them.

He would sometimes travel to Mass with Paddy and their wives in a horse and cart and on one Sunday after 11 o'clock mass, the horse bolted with the Dorans and Donoghues in the cart. Paddy recalled the sheer strength of Felix as he held the bolting horse and gradually brought him to a standstill on the street in Bodyke. He said he was one of the best horsemen he had ever encountered.

Paddy O' Donoughue and Mikey Doran Sr.
(Courtesy of Leo Rickard. Co Clare, 2010)

Barrell Top Wagon, typical mode of transport of Irish Travellers in the last century. (Courtesy of Tommy Fegan)

After travelling around Ireland for three decades, Felix and his family moved to Manchester in 1952, and Clare and Ireland lost a music icon and a legend. Ireland's loss was England's gain. Felix was faithful to the tradition handed down from the Cashes to the Dorans, and he ensured that future generations of the family would continue to be the standard bearers of this proud tradition.

It was a cold December morning in 2009 when the authors touched down at Manchester Airport. We were on our way to meet with Felix Doran's son Mikey Doran and his family, as part of our research for this book. Across the road from the Arrivals section of Manchester Airport stood a well-dressed, imposing figure and as he signalled us to cross the road to him, We were curious as to the kind of reception he would give us. We need not have worried, this was Felix Doran's son Mikey and after he introduced us to his handsome son Thomas, who was our driver, we were on our way, literally and metaphorically! We could never have anticipated the warm, friendly, generous and musical welcome about to unfold.

By the time we had reached our destination, a pub in Knutsford,

Cheshire, Mikey had already regaled us, with obvious pride, about his dad Felix Doran. He painted a picture of a generous, loving family man who provided very well for all his children, a man who taught them Christian values and a man who loved his family and cherished his Irish traditional music heritage.

"He was always a dealer, even if he had a drink or didn't have a drink he had a good head for business. He dealt in horses and feathers and nonferrous metals. That was a big rage at the time" (Mikey Doran, Dec 2009)

Felix was a strong, tall individual with a great sense of humor. He was loved the length and breadth of Manchester and its confines, and he was welcomed wherever he went. Stories regarding his generosity are legendary. Ena O'Brien, a wonderful accordionist who lives in Toronto, recounted the following story to the authors;

"Felix would visit my father's barber shop in Manchester in the 1960s to get his hair cut. My Dad would not take any money from him because he was Felix Doran the Piper. On one such visit Felix

Felix Doran playing music (Courtesy of Na Píobairí Uilleann)

46

went to his car and brought a banjo into the shop and gave it to my father as a token of his appreciation. That banjo now occupies a pride of place in this O'Brien's house in Toronto." Love, nor money couldn't buy that banjo as it is special because it was once owned by Felix Doran.

Sitting in the pub with Mikey Doran and his family on that December evening in 2009 was an enlightening experience. Mikey's sons listened to every word with awe as we recalled their grandfather's legacy to music in Ireland. We talked at length about his piping technique and his genius on the instrument. The younger members of the family had a sense of their grandfather's cult status, but clearly hung on to everything we recounted of the individual testimonies we related about their famous grandfather, and his iconic brother, Johnny. Mikey is an astute observer of traditional music and the Doran legacy, and he explained the intricacies of Felix's versions of tunes, most notably the *Fox Chase*, one of the most famous and most difficult pieces of Irish Music that Felix fashioned into his own, unmistakable version..

Discussing the Doran legend with members of Felix's extended family was an amazing experience. We were soon joined by Johnny Doran's grandson, Johnny Purcell, who arrived with his uilleann pipes ready to play for us. As the drink, teas and coffees flowed, Mikey Doran and Johnny Purcell got the piping session underway. Just when we thought it couldn't get any better, it did. The door of the pub opened and the larger-than-life John Rooney and his son Larry Rooney, both excellent pipers and both direct descendants of the Dorans, joined the session and raised the tempo even higher. The music was now reaching a crescendo and the icing on the cake happened when Mikey Doran Jr, Felix Doran's grandson, arrived and strapped on his Dave Williams' set of pipes and started to play. Five uilleann pipers of the Cash/Doran dynasty were in full flight in a small pub in Cheshire, evoking memories of the great John Cash, Johnny and Felix Doran. On this wintery Saturday evening, the music was wild, melodic, sweet, sorrowful and joyful.

The authors were awestruck with this incredible performance and hoped it would go on forever. Twelve hours later it was still going strong and by this time the pub was full of the Doran extended families who had now travelled from distances of up to 200 miles to be in attendance. They came from London, Oxford, Burton on Trent, Leicester, Luton and all over Manchester.

They were an amazing family and their hospitality knew no bounds. They could not do enough for us and we were particularly impressed with the younger generation of Dorans who were so aware of their grandfather's legacy and the kind of man he was. Bridget Doran, Felix's granddaughter wanted to know everything and she said at the end of the evening, "I am so proud of the Doran name" We thought it was a beautiful comment from a beautiful young woman. In the same spirit of pride, another little girl proudly proclaimed "I am a double Doran; my Daddy is a Doran and my Mummy is a Doran."

As the familiar tunes were played into the Manchester night, *Rakish Paddy, The Lark in the Morning* and *Coppers and Brass*, they brought the Doran Music to life in Felix's stomping ground in Manchester. The spirit of Felix and Johnny Doran was present on this night and we were honored to be present with them. There was no question of us staying in the local hotel that weekend. Even though the swelling numbers of the extended family arriving from throughout England put pressure on the accommodation available at the Doran boys' mobile homes, room was made for us. As we enjoyed a well-earned sleep on the crowded floor of the trailer, we experienced a sense of the closeness which is rarely available to non-Travellers. We have never experienced such generosity and hospitality.

In documenting the musical heritage of Felix Doran, it is important to also reflect on his lifestyle and his impact on people. There was definitely something different about the Dorans that set them apart from other Traveller families. They were always welcomed wherever they went in Ireland or England, they were taken into people's homes and people in a depressed Ireland gave them money willingly just to hear them play music.

Because Felix was such an imposing figure with dark, good looks he attracted a lot of female attention, but he was a devoted family man who was so proud of his family. His son Mikey recalled the TV footage that was recorded in Enniscorthy with the female ballad singer staring longingly at Felix as she sang Love is Teasing.
The Dorans are very closely knit and their pride in their heritage is evident. Because they have married within the wider family group

they are closely connected. The strong ties between the great musical dynasties of the Cash's, Rooneys, Purcells, McCanns and Murphys is deeply respected and cherished.

Legacy

While there is only one commercial recording of Felix's music, RTÉ and others also have archive material. As such, Felix is less of an enigma than his older brother, of whom there are only a few photographs and 10 tracks of recordings.

Together the two Doran brothers have made a very significant impact on the development of Irish traditional music. Johnny's music has had a profound impact on many of today's leading pipers, most notably Finbar Furey and Paddy Keenan directly and, through their influence, indirectly on many non-Traveller pipers, such as Davy Spillane and Michael 'Blackie' O'Connell, both living in County Clare.

Felix's music is remembered by many people still alive, and there is therefore more familiarity about him and his music. Many of the young generation of Traveller pipers today, such as Mikey Doran Jnr. and Larry Rooney, have inherited the jaunty, open and less complicated playing of Felix.

Felix Doran was an iconic figure in uilleann piping and he was master of his craft. His influence in Irish traditional music will be forever enshrined in the annals of music and he holds pride of place with Michael Coleman, Lad O'Byrne, Joe Cooley, John Cash, and all the other greats of a bygone golden era in Irish music.

The Doran Song
(Composed by Oliver O'Connell)

Oh the first time that I heard them play, at the Miltown Malbay fair
With their horses and their uilleann pipes, the Dorans came to Clare
We watched them playing on the street, on a cold September day
The crowds had gathered round to hear, the travelling Dorans play.
Johnny Doran was a travelling man, who roamed from town to town
From Killenaule to Donegal and from Clare to County Down
He played those pipes, the master's touch, we'll see his likes no more
The Doran boys though now long gone, are part of our folklore.
We listen to their favourite tunes, as they stood outside the door
Rakish Paddy and the Lark, and the Bucks of Oranmore
The pipers drones and the chanters tones, so haunting and so true
When Felix Doran played those pipes, he played for me and you.

The Doran sound is all around, just listen to the roar
When Paddy Keenan takes the stage, and he plays the Ballintore
Or Finbar's Lonesome Boatman, or the way he sings a song
The Keenans Fureys and the Dunnes, the legacy lives on.
I remember now of days gone by, and of times long long ago,
From the Ballylongford races, to the fairs at Ballinasloe
They stood on cold October streets, proud fathers and their sons
Listening to the music of the Dorans and the Dunnes.

The streets and lanes they are empty now, the pipers they are gone
No more we'll hear the Primrose Lass, or the haunting Slievenamon
The winters cold, it had taken hold, when Doran said goodbye
But we still hear the music of the black haired piper boy
We will never see their likes again, those travelling Doran boys.

Felix Doran headstone in Wicklow cemetery.
(Courtesy of Leo Rickard. 2001)

Chapter 4: The Fureys

"When the flag of Freedom was hoisted over Dublin Castle and Ireland was declared a Free State, there was nothing in the signed Treaty that said our new found freedom only applied to Irish people living in houses. This freedom also belonged to the Irish Traveller community who travelled all over Ireland keeping our heritage alive by their music, customs and culture." (Finbar Furey, 2009)

Two of the most famous pubs in Ireland where traditional music was encouraged and promoted were O'Donoghue's in Merrion Row, Dublin and O'Connor's pub in Doolin, Co Clare. O'D's, as the inner circle referred to it, was a musical and literary oasis from the late 1950s, surrounded by the hustle and bustle of nearby St Stephen's Green, Dáil Éireann and the Shelbourne Hotel. Doolin is a charming little village, tucked in between the roaring Atlantic and the majestic limestone Burren landscape. From Doolin's sea level location, the coastline rises to give way to the majestic cliffs of Moher. In the 1950s the immediate environment of both pubs could not have been more different, but in a strange way they were both the natural incubators for the phenomenon that was to become Irish traditional pubs, the place where traditional music, previously played in rural kitchens, was about to explode onto an unsuspecting global market.

Today, O'Donoghue's backroom is still small and narrow, with little natural light and where everyone is within an arm's reach of each other. In the 1950s, it was the perfect setting for five young men, attracted to each other through their love of folk and traditional music, to blend their individual styles into a worldwide brand that was to become the Dubliners.

Ted Furey

In 1958 Ted Furey had been invited by John Molloy, an actor who frequented the bar, to play music in the pub. Ted brought his 11-year-old son, Finbar back with him on his regular visits to play music. They were soon joined by Ciarán Burke, (one of the founder members of the Dubliners) and others. Burke was anxious to learn to play the tin whistle, and he subsequently visited the Furey's house in Ballyfermot to take lessons from the young Finbar. Ted was a permanent fixture in O'D's in the 1960s and 1970s.

Kieran Kelly was a radio operator in the Greek merchant navy in the early 1960s, and he often travelled back to Dublin to visit his parents. He would frequent O'Donoghue's Pub in Merrion Row on each of those trips and he speaks lovingly of his memory of Ted Furey in O'Donoghue's;

"One of the loveliest musicians ever to play in this pub was Ted Furey (I believe that he actually spells his name Furey) the father of the famous Furey brothers. Ted was a gentleman of the old school. During the years that I knew him, I don't believe that I ever heard him use bad language of any kind. He would come into the pub, find himself a nice corner, take out his fiddle and play all night. He certainly knew at least 200 different tunes and during the night he would play requests for other patrons in the pub. This always kept the Guinness flowing like the Mississippi towards his table and any friend who was lucky enough to be at that table were encouraged by Ted to get rid of the surplus, and at the end of the night, having kept everyone in the pub entertained and kept them drinking, the owner of the pub would give Ted 10 cigarettes and his bus fare home. I know this because Ted told me and in fact I witnessed Ted receiving the bounty. At the time I drove a little white sports car called an Austin Healey, just a two seat vehicle with low seats that gave the impression of speed. Many a night I drove Ted home to the Spanish Lady, as he called his wife, and several times I shared a fish stew with him". (Kelly, K. Dublin, 1993)

Around the same time in O'Connor's pub in Doolin, Co Clare, the local Russell brothers, Pakie, Micho and Gussy and the Killoughry brothers, John and Paddy, held court every night playing Irish

traditional music, bringing this pub to international recognition. Ted Furey, the patriarch of the world famous Furey Brothers, who were pioneers in bringing Irish music to an international audience, was a regular participant in these historic gatherings, encouraging a trend that continues to draw thousands of visitors from every part of the globe to this picturesque village in the shadows of the majestic Cliffs of Moher.

Just as the Doran brothers did, Ted loved Co Clare with a passion and he was hugely respected all over the county. It was ironic that in 1979 he actually suffered a massive heart attack and died in Doolin while on one of his regular visits to Co Clare.

Ted Furey's father, Martin Furey, who played whistle and uilleann pipes, was from outside Salthill in Co Galway. Little wonder, then, that Galway, and particularly Connemara, was a favorite stomping ground for Ted as he busked all over this wind swept landscape. If

Doolin, Co Clare, 2011 (Courtesy Mark Larkin)

Previous page; Ted Furey, father of The Furey brothers
(Courtesy of Finbar Furey)

you listen closely to Finbar Furey playing a slow air on the uilleann pipes, you can hear that West Galway blás that only Connemara inhabitants have; it is soulful, sean nós that sears into the soul of the listener. The sea and the islands play a very important role in Finbar's compositions and of course his *Lonesome Boatman* is a piece of music that has never been equalled for its depth and soul. In spite of countless musicians all over the world playing this tune, only Finbar can play it the way it should be played. These influences most definitely have come from Ted, and his father Martin Furey, who were Galway natives with a grá for the barren countryside of Connemara. There are also influences in Finbar's slow airs of the iconic Connemara singer Seosaimh Ó'Heanaí.

The Fury Brothers

The four Furey brothers Finbar George, Eddie and Paul (RIP) - were born and reared in 116, Claddagh Road, Ballyfermot in Dublin. Their father Ted originally came from the Salthill area of Galway and their mother, Nora, was from Kilfenora in Co Clare. From the time the boys were able to crawl, Ted made sure that they would play music and in hard, tough times in the 1950s and 60s when money was scarce, and employment opportunities were practically non existent for young men ,and young Traveller men inparticular, in Dublin's sprawling estates. The Furey brothers were coached in the art of music making by their father. Well aware of the opportunity to create a good living from playing Irish traditional music, Ted gave his sons a great start in life by instilling the discipline of learning and practicing their trade, and by providing them with the best available instruments. According to Finbar, the house was full of banjos, fiddles, guitars, and pipes.

Finbar recalls his father Ted one day telling a young 14 year- old enthusiast how to play music. He said music is like a flight of stairs "you run up three steps, back two, three up, back one, you dance four up, dance two back, you never get to the top and you never get to the bottom. Playing Irish music is like dancing up and down the stairs. Listen to Doran, he never seems to finish the tune and its always different, you can never measure it, what a fantastic piper"
Ted travelled with the legendary Johnny Doran, Felix Doran and the Dunne brothers from Limerick. His close friend, John Keenan,

a fellow Traveller piper who also passed on to his sons and their families a rich musical heritage, often embarked on fishing expeditions together. Busking was an important activity for them, and because of the style, vitality and tempo of their music, they were able to provide sufficient money to feed the families.

The close bond of the Traveller musicians in the Ireland of the 1950s, 1960s and 1970s was truly special. The Furey, Doran, Keenan and the Dunne families were not the only Irish Travellers who played Irish traditional music for a living. (The Raineys in Connemara and Dohertys in Donegal were playing their music and plying their wares around the same time). They kept in touch with each other, often camping together, borrowing musicians from the other families when the need arose, exchanging tunes and alerting each other to the dangers and opportunities to be encountered in various towns and villages around the country. Mickey, Christy, Joseph and Paddy Dunne often played and swapped tunes with Ted Furey.

A complex and secret set of messages was developed to indicate where families had been, and where they were going. For example, a stone in a stone wall would be adjusted in a certain manner to indicate which family had passed by, when they had done so, and to where they were going.

Ted was a charismatic character whose presence lit up a room when he walked in. Oliver O'Connell can remember clearly in the early 1970s walking into the Roadside Tavern in Lisdoonvarna in Co Clare, a great pub for Irish music whose owner Mrs Curtin encouraged people to play in her premises. "It attracted the greats of Irish music at the time, Micilín Conlon, Tommy Peoples, Micho Russell. Ted Furey always called in when he was in Clare. On this particular evening, Ted was in the corner "holding court" with an attentive audience and his fiddle was our welcoming beacon on the approach to the pub. He was truly amazing to watch as he went through *The Wheels of the World* and *The Dawn* with extraordinary finger work. A superb musician by any standard." (O'Connell, O. Ennis, 2009)

There was also a wonderful story told of a horse fair in Maam Cross in Connemara in the late 1960s. In what was not an unusual event in those days, a fight broke out, an event that would have been relished

Ted Furey
(Courtesy of Comhaltas Ceoltóirí Éireann)

by the local boys at the time. At some point during the fist fight, Ted Furey started playing the fiddle in the style well suited to competing with noisy, outdoor distractions. Almost instantly the fight stopped as everyone gathered round to hear this white-bearded figure playing some beautiful airs. The story goes that both protagonists in the earlier melee were seen standing side by side listening to Ted Furey playing Irish music on that Connemara roadside.

Ted travelled extensively throughout Ireland, and his arrival in Mark's Bar in Dundalk, Co Louth was greeted with great excitement when he visited. Mark's was one of the earliest session pubs in Ireland, second only to O'Donoghues in Dublin, and O'Connor's pub in Doolin. Hard pressed nationalists from nearby Northern Ireland crossed the border nightly in the early days of the troubles to seek respite from the unfolding crisis. The sight of the flamboyant Furey, in full flight with resident fiddler Peter McArdle, was enough to raise the spirits of the weary northerners. For various reasons, Mark's bullet-proof door (which was a prison cell door, complete with spy-hole) was always locked, even early in the evening when there was no-one in the bar. Admission could only be gained by delivery of a secret tap of a coin on the stain glassed windows, and even regulars would be anxious to see if they could gain entrance. The expectation of a great night's music compensated for the long wait, but the unmistakable strains of Furey's fiddle playing, discernible as the inside door opened, raised the expectations even higher. Ted's sons were also embraced warmly by the musical fraternity of north Louth and south Armagh.

"One Saturday afternoon, in October, 1972, one of the most violent years of the Northern troubles, I hitchhiked with Ted's son Paul (RIP) from Dublin to Dundalk; we were on our way to Mark's Bar. Paul was a wonderful accordion player and I witnessed the reaction from musicians and regulars at the anticipation of a performance from one of the Fureys. We eventually arrived in Mark's around 10 o'clock, after a few liquid distractions en route, just as Peter McArdle and the local musicians were cranking the session up a notch or two. Between the door and the musicians' table, barely 5 steps, Paul had discarded the accordion case and was joining the locals in a rousing version of *Toss the Feathers*, one of Ted's. That instantly accounted for another two notches! His banter, wit, and storytelling were in as much demand as his driving, attacking accordion playing. Paul showed no hesitation at moving on later that night to a Shebeen in South Armagh, at a time when most southerners would not consider crossing the border to any part of the north, and least of all to so-called "Bandit Country" in South Armagh. The Mark's Bar welcome

Paul Furey and his mother Nora, Dublin, 1965.
(Courtesy of Alen MacWeeney)

was repeated all over again!" (Fegan, T. Camlough, 2010).

In the1950s and 1960s Irish Travellers were welcomed in areas isolated from the mainstream of news, products, services and social entertainment. Traveller musicians, such as the Fureys, were particularly welcomed by local musicians and dancers because they provided the excuse for enlivened dancing and music making and they brought eagerly awaited new tunes to the locality, and, in turn, they picked up local tunes and brought them to other areas in Ireland on their itineraries. Ted Furey's sons benefited from this education on the road, immersed in influences from a wide geographic location and regional styles that would not have been available to most traditional musicians in the settled community, who, through lack of opportunity, mobility or finance, rarely ventured outside their own locality at that time.

In later years Ted Fureys four sons, along with Davy Arthur, surpassed even his high expectations as they became household names all over the world, playing to packed houses in London's Albert Hall, New York's Carnegie Hall and the Sydney Opera House.

In the 1960s Finbar and Eddie Furey blazed a trail across Europe, bringing a new sound with pipes and guitar that has stood the test of time. Other iconic bands such as Planxty and the Bothy Band were undoubtedly influenced by the Fureys, and today, over forty years later, we can hear the Furey sound in most of the emerging new folk and traditional groups. The Furey brothers sowed the seed and raised the bar for those who followed in their footsteps.

Finbar also recalled himself and Eddie on the folk circuit in Europe in the 1960s and 1970s, and when they received the kind of reaction to their music from German, Scottish, and French audiences, they knew they had something unique and special.

The two brothers won three sections of the Rose of Tralee International Festival in the 1960s-the Main event, the Pub event and the Street event. Sensing that the popularity of their music could transport itself well outside Ireland, they moved to Edinburgh, initially staying in a commune-type house run by Diane Halley. This house was a stopping off point for the Clancy Brothers, The Dubliners, Billy Connolly, Gerry Rafferty and others. The young Fureys immersed themselves in other musical influences which later found expression in their future developments. They built up a strong following in folk clubs and universities, and eventually demand for their lively performances brought them to bigger venues throughout Europe. They later played with the Clancy brothers, culminating in a sellout concert in New York's Carnegie Hall.

The Furey Brothers and Davy Arthur band was formed in 1978, and they were the group that everyone wanted to hear throughout Ireland, as they packed venues with energetic performances that defined this golden era of Irish Folk music.

In 1978 when the *Green Fields of France* hit the No. 1 spot on the Irish charts, The Fureys were appearing in Shannon in Co Clare, and the demand for tickets was such that a queue formed at 5 o'clock in the afternoon. They were not due on stage until 10 o'clock. Patrons waited for 5 hours to hear them.

Such was the influence of the group on Irish folk music that today songs like *Sweet Sixteen, From Clare to Here, Red Rose Café* and *Green Fields of France* have stood the test of time and have been adopted by another generation.

In 1998 the Fureys were awarded a Certificate of Appreciation from the Australian Songwriters' Association. Finbar left the Group to pursue a very successful solo career in 1996. On Sunday, June 16th 2002 Paul Furey died at the age of 52 years. Ar dheis Dé go raibh a anam cheolmhar.

The Group with George and Eddie and some members of the extended family are going as strong as ever on the ballad and folk circuit. Finbar has added acting to his eclectic portfolio with an exuberant delivery of *New York Girls* in Martin Scorsese's *Gangs of New York* with Leonardo Di Caprio and Daniel Day Lewis. Finbar's son Martin is a member of the very successful High Kings ballad group currently performing to audiences all over the world

The Furey household in Ballyfermot was a magical place to be in the 1960s with great musicians calling to play tunes with Ted. The Keenans lived close by, and these two incredible music families bonded together as they developed their skills and repertoire in preparation for their destiny to make an indelible mark on Irish music. Finbar

and Eddie loved all kinds of music, Rock-n-Roll, Jazz, Blues and Trad. They were quite adept at incorporating other forms of music into their sets when playing to different audiences, accounting for their meteoric rise in popularity throughout Europe.

The Fureys have made a significant contribution to the development of Irish music over the last 50 years. Ted Furey and other Traveller musicans made a valuable contribution to sustaining Irish music at a time when it was in danger of being considerably marginalized. During the 1930s and 1940s emigration, the austerity of World War II and other social factors were contributing to the music's demise in Ireland. Against this very tough economic background Irish music was not a priority with many in the settled community, who were now focusing on providing for their children in harsh times.

The Fureys and their fellow Travellers ensured that the music survived and flourished through their visits to isolated communities, desperate for respite from the tough times. Ted Furey and his sons gave them that respite through their music, song and storytelling.

There is today a lot of focus on the Traveller style of playing music which is a distinctive art form. Finbar prefers to think of it as more of a heritage that has been handed down from his ancestors and does not agree with putting a label on it. However he recognizes that there is something special and unique in it but it is the Irish that makes it so special.

He also believes that we as a nation lost out on a very important part of our culture when some of our best players from the Traveller community were never recorded.

"We had people who were paid by our State Broadcasting company to go out into the highways and bye ways of Ireland and record Irish artists for our archives, Wonderful idea, but they passed by the caravans on the side of the road where the most incredible music was being played and no one called to record them, what a loss for Ireland." (Furey, F. Dublin, 2009)

The Furey family were definitely an iconic musical institution in Irish culture and the fact that one house in Dublin's Ballyfermot produced a family of musicians, singers, composers, poets, actors, multi-instrumentalists, who captivated global audiences with their brand of Irish music at a time in Ireland when there was no Arts Council, no grants, no scholarships, no world music academy,, no encouragement and no help from anyone, speaks volumes for the depth of talent that this family had. The Furey brothers, with their unique and fresh arrangements awakened in audiences throughout Ireland, and amongst the Irish Diaspora a renewed sense of identity that had been long suppressed. And it ignited a love for our culture and our national identity through the music they played.

In spite of their phenomenal global success, they never lost touch with their roots, consistently acknowledging Ted as their main influence. Ted Furey and his four sons have produced over fifty recordings ranging from Irish traditional dance music, traditional and contemporary folk songs, and popular music. The musical

Above: Paul, Finbar, Ted and Eddie Furey(missing form the picture George Furey) (Courtesy of Alen MacWeeney. Dublin Hills, Circa 1965)

Next Page: Finbar Furey holding the box fiddle, made by his dad Ted Furey (Courtesy of Tommy Fegan)

inventiveness even embraced the Hollywood film industry, with the production of *The Fureys Sing Chaplin*, (Brud Records, 2002), a tribute the Furey Brothers made to the remarkable song writing skills of Charlie Chaplin. Finbar and Eddie were amongst the early pioneers of Irish traditional and Folk music throughout Europe, cultivating a new audience from which many subsequent Irish musicians would benefit. In England, they raised the profile of Irish music at a time when stereotypes, fuelled by anti-Irish sentiments at the height of the Troubles, portrayed Irish music as bawdy ballads in beer-filled bars. Their popularizing of anti-war and antiviolence sentiments in songs such as *The Green Fields of France*, helped give expression to the frustration of endless international conflicts which formed the backdrop to the Fureys' musical careers, ranging from Vietnam, Northern Ireland, and the Middle East.

When Finbar Furey and his brothers appeared on the Top of the Pops singing *Sweet Sixteen*, others began to appreciate that Ireland had something that was special. They were amongst the earliest pioneers in the global branding of Irish culture, a trend that continues unabated almost 50 years later. Riverdance has many tributaries, and one of them can be sourced back to that overcrowded house in Ballyfermott, in the early 1950s.

Their Music and Their Legacy

After Ted Furey's death, Finbar, encouraged by his mother, investigated the contents of a suitcase of Ted's music in the attic, and discovered the words and music to *When You Were Sweet Sixteen* which Ted often sang. His mother encouraged him to record the song, but Finbar protested, saying, 'That's not a folk song.' His mother reprimanded him; 'How dare you! That song was written by a fellow called John Thornton in 1847, at the time of the famine. He left Ireland on a famine boat with his young wife, from Tipperary. Now if that's not a folk song after that, I don't know what is.'

Finbar Furey's sensitivity to a good song whose time had come was at work early in his musical career. His version of a song his friend Gerry Rafferty gave to him, *Her Father Didn't Like Me Anyway*, was hugely popular in Britain. So much so that in 1972, John Peel, the influential disc jockey, placed the Furey's song ahead of the Beatles'

Get Back as the most popular song of the year. Peel also proclaimed Finbar and Eddie Furey as The Best Act of the Year, and in doing so instantly opened up Irish folk music to a wider audience, which was neither Irish nor folk-inclined. The Fureys were connecting Irish Folk and Traditional music to the broader British pop culture in a way that no other Irish performers had done before. They went on to repeat this connection years later with *When You Were Sweet Sixteen*. A cover version of *Her Father Didn't Like Me Anyway*, recorded by Shane McGowan and the Popes in 1994 (ZTT Records) is further evidence of the enduring appeal of the song.

The selection of songs, tunes and instruments on Finbar and Eddie's first two recordings on the Transatlantic label, *Finbar and Eddie Furey* (1968) and *The Lonesome Boatman* (1969), very much set a new direction and precedent that would be further developed by Irish Folk and Traditional groups such Planxty and the Bothy Band in the early 1970's, and by many more popular Folk and Traditional groups in Ireland, Europe and the USA to this day. The arrangement of *The Flowers in the Valley* (Finbar and Eddie Furey,1968) is an outstanding example of the deployment of the full potential the uilleann pipes offer in song accompaniment. In this version, the drones set a steady, melancholic mood in anticipation of Eddie's plaintive vocal rendering. Finbar engages regulator notes and chords in advance of chanter accompaniment in a relentless exploration of different harmonies, intriguing but not distracting.

The McPeake's family group in Belfast had also been applying uilleann pipe accompaniment to folksongs around the same time, but the Furey Brothers unleashed the power and potential of the pipe's harmonics, sympathetic to the mood and meaning of each song, and constrained enough to allow guitar accompaniment to seek a similar complement to the lyrics. And, aided by influential commentators such as John Peel, they successfully brought Irish traditional music to wider audiences abroad, and in Ireland.

Low D whistle

In 1967, when Finbar and Eddie were living in Coventry, England, Finbar accidently broke the Indian bamboo whistle which was a central feature of the Furey's sound. In desperation, he approached a friend, Bernard Oveton (1930-2008), a welder by trade, and asked him to design a similar whistle from an aluminum tube. The result was the creation of the Overton Low D whistle, a standard instrument in almost every Irish and English folk and traditional group in the world, and the industry standard for low D whistle and manufacturers worldwide. The distinctive flat sides of the whistle at the mouthpiece arose when Finbar's then young son, Martin, accidentally dropped a heavy weight on whistle, and that feature has stayed with the Overton Low D whistle ever since.

Ted Furey, his sons Finbar, Eddie, George and Paul (RIP) lit the flame for Irish Traditional and Folk music in the 1960s passing on a great tradition to Irish audiences all over the world, and they undoubtedly made a very significant contribution to the healthy traditional music scene that we take so much for granted today.

The infulence of Finbar Furey's on Ciaran Burke of the Dubliners and Roy Williamson of the Corries was central to the sound of two of Ireland's and Scotland's leading folk groups. Finbar and Eddie added to the Clancy Brothers' sound when they performed and recorded with them in 1979. Dave Stewart of the Eureythmics, was taught to play the guitar by Finbar when he stayed with Finbar and Eddie after running away from home in the 1960s.

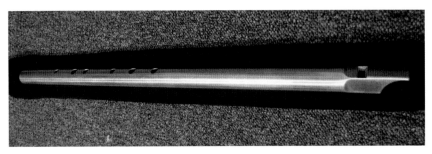

Low D whistle (Courtesy of Mark Larkin)

O'Donoughue' Pub (Courtesy of Kglavin)

Paul and Finbar Furey
(Courtesy of Sheila Furey)

O'Donoughue's Pub

O'Donoghue's Pub in Merrion Row, Dublin hosts music sessions seven nights a week, and its walls are covered by hundreds of photographs of the many famous musicians who played there over the past 40 years. The biggest photograph by far is the giant almost life size photograph of Finbar and Eddie Furey just inside the front door on the left. The stature and prominence of the picture seems to symbolize the importance of this music family to the development of our musical heritage.

"I can sit down and play music on the street and not feel ashamed of busking for a meal if I had to for my family. I have no feeling about being a superstar or travelling the world, I did it all and I brought my Ireland with me, I enjoyed it and I was proud of the tradition" (Finbar Furey, 2009)

Ted Furey, Fiddle, Frank McNamara Banjo, and the dog. (Courtesy of Frank McNamara)

George Furey

"I suppose I was a bit eager and impetuous to show off when I was young. We all are at times but I learned to be humble. I was told by my father to always be humble." (George Furey, German magazine ,Circa 1970s)

Chapter 5: The Keenans

An Extraordinary Musical Dynasty

The Keenans were another musical Irish Traveller family who, like the Fureys, settled into Ballyfermot around the 1950s, and both families, and their sons, developed social, musical and friendship bonds which helped shape the direction and popularity of Irish traditional music over the succeeding decades.

In Dublin in the late 1960s and early 1970s, a vibrant, exciting phase of Irish folk and traditional music was getting underway. The Fureys, Dubliners and the Keenans were prominent in the largely urban-based revival, while Seán Ó'Riada and his protégées in Ceoltóirí Chualann and the Chieftains were experimenting on the edge of the traditional boundaries, and presenting new sounds to an eager audience. Then along came Planxty, pushing the possibilities of instrumental backing within the genre just like Finbar and Eddie Furey had done in the early 60s. Planxty brought the sound of the uilleann pipes to a new, younger urban-based audience. This was a new sound, controversial to the ears of some purists, but with the imprimatur of others, such as Séamus Ennis, mentor to Liam O Floinn, Planxty's uilleann piper.

Balladeers like Paddy Reilly, Jim McCann and Danny Doyle were packing in crowds in the Old Shelling in Dublin, operated by the irrepressible Bill Fuller. Criss-crossing the Atlantic during these decades, Tommy Makem and the Clancy Brothers were maintaining the traditional approach to ballad singing, which depended on good, old-fashioned vocal harmonies, with minimum instrumentation. The Embankment in Tallaght was the folk Mecca of the era, most memorable for the concerts which hosted the Bothy Band, an exciting new format of Irish traditional music, in which Paddy Keenan also awakened in many, for the first time, an appreciation of the music of the uilleann pipes.

O'Donoughue's Pub in Merrion Row, Dublin, was gaining national prominence as a venue for consistent, good quality, informal traditional music sessions. Ted McKenna was singing traditional songs of the working classes, honoring Larkin, Pearse and Connolly

Above: Paddy Kenan and John Keenan Sr
Left; Paddy and his brother Johnny Keenan and friends.
1967 Dublin (Courtesy of Alen MacWeeney)

and, with ironic paradox, infusing English ballads and sea shanties into the national repertoire. The sound of Paddy Keenan's Irish uilleann pipes, accompanying English sea shanties, such as *Go to Sea No More,* with Paul Furey's sensitive and evocative Paolo Soprano accordion accompaniment, was the stuff of unrehearsed improvisation- nightly features in Paddy O'Donoghue's small back room in the early 1970s. At the same time, and often on the same night, legendary musicians like Séamus Ennis, Tommy Peoples, and Seán Keane were likely to drop in for a tune with resident musicians John Kelly and Joe Ryan, exiles from Clare, keeping the "drop pure" up at the front of the bar.

Across town, in Slattery's in Capel Street, one could walk in any night and be totally enchanted by some of the best music ever heard. On the stage on some of those nights, the Pavees, a raw, exciting traditional group led by John Keenan and his sons Brendan, Thomas, Paddy and Johnny, were in full swing. Guesting with the Keenans on different nights were singers and musicians of the calibre of Liam

Weldon, George and Paul Furey, Seán Garvey, Paddy Glackin and others.

One of the most memorable traditional recordings was a duet produced in the 1970s by Paddy Keenan and Paddy Glackin, simply called *Doublin*. This recording has stood the test of time and is a constant reference CD for aspiring young pipers and fiddle players. Glackin is a Dub, of Donegal extraction, while Keenan's Traveller roots are in Dublin, yet their music and backgrounds fused harmoniously, producing an awesome synergy that was magical to

John Sr, Paddy and Johnny Keenan

hear. Another aspect of this wonderful recording was the tight playing of both men; one from a Traveller background and the other from the settled community. Their music had resonances of Doran and Clancy playing together, or the Raineys and the Keanes of Galway. No prejudices here, just music binding together the two traditions. Oliver O'Connell's first encounter with the Keenan family took place in 1974 in Lisdoonvarna, Co Clare. He well remembers a session in which crowds were packed in like sardines. In Ireland in 1974, fire regulations were practically non-existent, so you could have three times the legal crowd limit packed into the lounge bar for the wild music sessions that were so much in vogue at that time.

"Suddenly, without warning, we heard the sound of the uilleann pipes in a far corner of the bar; first the continuous hum of the drones, and then the magical melody played on the chanter by a tall figure, surrounded by an adoring crowd, head bowed, hair flowing down at either side of his features, and music just flowing out like an Amazonian waterfall." (Oliver O'Connell, 2010)

The audience in the packed lounge that night was spellbound by the lonesome piper as he gave full vent to the tunes he played. It was the first time O'Connell had heard *Colonel Frazer*, one of the 'big' reels to be found in the repertoire of most Irish Traveller musicians. On this night, to an unsuspecting audience, it was unleashed by Paddy

Paddy Keenan in full flight in Carlingford, 2010. (Courtesy of Tommy Fegan)

Keenan. Like countless others that night, O'Connell was hooked on the sound of the pipes, played in a style not known to many, an Irish Travellers' style of piping, traceable back to the early 19th century, to John Cash, the Traveller horse-dealer from Wexford who was the patriarch of the Doran dynasty.

There was something so special in the music Keenan produced; his whole persona had a mystique, both in terms of his appearance and his undoubted skill on the pipes. Paddy had developed a cult following in the early 1970s, and people flocked to any venue where he was playing. The famous Bothy Band was just taking a hold on the Irish traditional music scene at that time, and Paddy was crucial to their new sound. Paddy was a member of a very musical family, and his siblings were accomplished musicians.. Their father, John Keenan, was born in Co Westmeath and he married Mary Bravender from Cavan. They had four sons, Paddy, Johnny, Brendan and Thomas and two daughters, Eileen and Angela.

The Keenan clan moved into 116, Oranmore Road, Ballyfermot, Dublin sometime around 1958, in close proximity to the Fureys, who

John Keenan Sr and Paddy Keenan, Dublin, 1967. (Courtesy of Alen MacWeeney)

Bothy Band, 1970s. Kevin Burke, Triona Ni Dhonaill, Paddy Keenan, Donal Lunny, Micheal O' Dhonaill and Matt Molloy.

were living in nearby 116, Claddagh Road. The bond of friendship between Ted Furey and John Keenan was very close; both men were musicians, they enjoyed fishing, a few pints and they each had four sons steeped in the Traveller music culture. The Keenan and Furey boys to this day are as close as any family, and Finbar refers to the Keenans as his brothers.

Paddy is the most prominent member of the Keenan Family, due initially to his critical role in the iconic Bothy Band of the 1970s. The Bothy Band burst onto the Irish traditional music scene in 1974, and for the few short years that they were in existence they raised the tempo to a breathtaking level and introduced a new template for tune arrangements that continue to be the standard for emerging new groups. Their unique, exhilarating sound was driven by its three lead players; Matt Malloy, Tommy Peoples and Paddy Keenan, while Donal Lunny, Micheál and Tríona Ní Dhomhnaill provided the strong rhythm and accompaniment which was so distinctive and unique. They brought traditional music to new heights, as far as the tradition would allow, teasingly close to rock 'n' roll, without diluting its integrity. But most agree that it was Keenan's pulsating, attacking sound on the uilleann pipes that set the Bothies in a league of their own. Nearly 40 years later, Keenan continues to mesmerize crowds with his inimitable, unique Traveller style of uilleann piping.

"I met with him after one of his excellent gigs in Dolan's in Limerick in 2010 and while in the 1970s Paddy did not talk much, nowadays he is a great communicator, and always eager to share his experiences."(O'Connell, O. Ennis, 2009)

Paddy talks openly about his three brothers, Brendan, Tommy, his late brother Johnny Keenan and his dad John Keenan, who was a multi-instrumentalist and played the pipes. Paddy maintains that if his dad concentrated on the pipes he would have been a brilliant piper. He also spoke lovingly of his dad's friendship with Ted Furey and recalled how they would spend their time fishing and busking. Paddy has boundless respect and admiration for Finbar Furey and talks of Finbar's skill on the uilleann pipes, and of the wonderful childhood they shared.

The Keenan patriarch, John Keenan, knew and played with Johnny Doran. They camped, worked and played together. Keenan subsequently was determined that he would have a piper in the family, such was his infatuation with Doran. He designated Paddy as the piper, but Paddy readily admits that his brother Johnny was a better piper. The Doran mantle, however, fell to Paddy, simply because Johnny was quicker on his feet at getting out to play when practice time came around in the Keenan household. Johnny was not prepared to dedicate the time required to learn the intricacies of the instrument.

Old John Keenan was a tough task master, particularly where music was concerned, and he could not understand why a learner could not get it right first time. "You would get a slap from him if you got it wrong" Paddy recalled. "Those were the times that were in it, you got slapped in school, and you got slapped at home, you were given a hard upbringing because you had to be tough in the Pavee world". (Keenan, P. Dublin, 2010)

Johnny Keenan

As part of our research for this publication, we inquired about other dominant Traveller families, and Paddy remembered the Keenans, Joyces, McDonaghs, Maughans, and McCanns.

The bigger the family name the more powerful they were. "This is what we were brought up to face and be prepared for," he said, " so the uilleann pipes was going to be my ticket, and my dad disciplined me, while my brothers now had more freedom to go out and play, I was the piper and Johnny was a banjo player, and a great player.

I remember Johnny used to prop me up on the bed and play the banjo for me. Great memories. He was an excellent musician. You could put Johnny sitting at a piano and leave him there for half an hour and when you came back, he could play it. He started off playing the fiddle. I remember in the 1960s a professor from Paris knocking on our door in Ballyfermot and talking to my dad about taking Johnny to Paris for formal musical education. My dad would not let him go, unfortunately. So sad. He was gifted, very talented." (Keenan, P. 2010)

Johnny Keenan and his daughter Elizabeth. (Courtesy of Chris Keenan)

Johnny played pipes, fiddle, banjo, guitar and accordion. John Keenan Sr played music with Ted Furey and Pecker Dunne. Pecker, who was a regular visitor in every town in Ireland at the time, used the thimble for strumming the banjo, just as Johnny Keenan did. They played music regularly around Dublin and they travelled long distances to places like Co Clare, where they were guaranteed a huge welcome and would be feted like kings, simply because of the music.

Johnny was a regular feature of Co Clare's vibrant music scene in the 1970s. Today, he is lovingly remembered by such greats as Michael Hynes, Christy Barry, Kevin Griffin and Michael Kelleher, music legends still carrying on a great music tradition in north Clare. They all agree that Johnny was an exceptional musician and he is held in very high esteem by everyone who knew him.

Johnny's wife, Chris Keenan, recalls Johnny's generosity to young aspiring musicians who attended his Dublin sessions in O'Donoghue's. It didn't matter to Johnny who was playing; he would always make room for young or inexperienced musicians. When Johnny passed away in March, 2000, St Mel's Church in Longford was packed to capacity with people from all over the world who came to pay their respects. Chris Keenan remembers clearly the number of musicians who approached her and said how grateful they were to Johnny for giving them their music break by allowing them to play with musicians of his calibre in Dublin in the 1970s and 1980s. Johnny will be remembered fondly by his loving family circle, and legions of music lovers. And his pioneering style of using the thimble instead of a plectrum made that unique sound that will never be forgotten.

Chris also recalled how Johnny, even though he was the smallest of the Keenan family, would stand up to his dad John Sr and verbally take him on, and she said his dad loved that challenge from 'this little squirt.'

Chris spoke of Johnny's love for Gerry O'Connor and Barney McKenna, two of Ireland's greatest banjo players. She also paid tribute to Johnny for his decision to get his life in order when they lived in Longford. He loved the countryside and he loved nature, but he showered the most love and attention on his little daughter Elizabeth, the apple of his eye, now a beautiful young woman who took her Leaving Certificate Examination in June 2011. Elizabeth was just 7 years old when Johnny passed away on the 27th March in 2000 from lung cancer.

The Johnny Keenan Banjo Festival, held every year in Longford, is now an international event, attracting the top names in the world of banjo playing to this Midlands town. Masters of the banjo, such as Gerry O'Connor, Enda Scahill and John Carty play in session in the town and in the many concerts organized during the event. The Festival has also attracted some of the world's leading exponents of 4 string and 5 string banjo playing a truly fitting memorial to a wonderful musician from a talented family.

The Fureys were living in Ballyfermot before the Keenans moved in sometime in the 1950s. Paddy recalled the sense of musical exploration and collaboration between the two families;

"In 1959 Finbar Furey moved in to live with us and it was bedlam after that. Any chance of a decent education went out the window, as we would be playing music until all hours of the morning. My dad was in his element. We were blowing chanters and whistles constantly. I would be up listening to this constant music, Johnny strumming along to my dad, and also Tommy Ryan would arrive, the only man with a tape recorder and we would have a great session. We were up until 6 o'clock in the morning and then we had to go to school. Our house got the name 'Radio 116 Oranmore Road'. We had to make quiet reeds for the pipes because the neighbours were complaining about the noise." (Keenan, P. Dublin, 2010)

The Keenan household in Oranmore Road, Ballyfermot was a virtual traditional music paradise, with Brendan, Thomas, Paddy, Johnny and John Sr and Finbar Furey playing incredible Irish music together, for days at a time. Brendan and Thomas Keenan still live in Ballyfermot. Both men are excellent uilleann pipers and fantastic whistle players. All the brothers recognize the unique musical heritage they inherited from their dad, John Sr. The Keenans' mother was Mary Bravender and she played a little on the accordion, and the Keenan sisters Angela and Eileen also played whistles.

Paddy Keenan

Paddy Keenan talked about the difference in the music that was played by people who were of a Traveller background. Paddy attributed the difference to the respective contexts of lifestyles of Travellers and settled people; "Music brings out the difference because music is a mood and you reflect the mood in your music sorrow, pain, rejection, hardship. It has to come out and music is the vehicle to project those emotions."

He stated that if he was asked to play like somebody else he could probably do it, but he said that not everyone could play like he plays, unless they have experienced what he has experienced. (Mickey Dunne makes a similar point in his description of the Travellers'style of playing, in Chapter 7)

"I was at a wedding recently in Inisbofin and I played with Liam Ó'Floinn. We played nice music, and then when I played on my own, my mood kicked in and the music was different."

Paddy went on to talk about the young musicians today and mentioned in particular Michael O'Connell from Co Clare who, he observed, has incredible execution, ornamentation and control of the pipes, an outstanding musician in his opinion. He also mentioned that there are several other young pipers who have a mature mood in their playing, and that you can see how they were influenced by Johnny Doran. Paddy confirmed that Johnny Doran was the greatest influence of all time on his playing. He also has a high regard for Felix Doran's piping, and he is delighted about the number of young pipers today who want to do what the Dorans were doing.

Paddy is flattered that there are young pipers now who model their playing on his, and he hopes that this will help them learn how to turn the tune in different directions.

"This will be fantastic for them in later years when they have developed their own style and moods and can incorporate these extras into their playing. These technical embellishments are useful when not overdone, and can add something extra to the playing. I remember teaching a class when I was in my thirties, and a little boy about 11 years old made a little mistake and he blushed because he was playing for me. That night I was playing and I used his mistake, which became a very effective ornamentation. Someone pointed out that I did not play it like that today, and I said 'I know, I got that note from that little boy.' Well, he went crimson with embarrassment, but the note worked in the right context. His note was a mistake but I gave it back to him as an add-on to his playing.

Paddy says "No" to The Beatles

Paddy went to London in the late 1960s and took a break from the music for three years;
"I played guitar and sang and busked in London. It was a hippy world at the time. I tried to pawn my pipes one time but eventually gave them to a friend because there was a certain embarrassment in being part of this hippy world. I spent a lot of time busking and singing on the London underground.

Paddy & Johnny Keenan. 1967 (Courtesy of Alen MacWeeney)

The Beatles were in vogue and their management made contact with me; they wanted a new sound and the pipes were a possibility, and someone had told them that I was a piper who would be suitable for this new sound.

Grattan Puxton was the head of the World Gypsy Association and his wife was involved in the Beatles' management, and they were sending a Limo for me in London and I walked away from it "I'm still walking away" he said with a hearty laugh. (Keenan, P. Dublin, 2010)

Paddy decided the morning of the rehearsals in Abbey Road with the Beatles that he would go off busking in the Underground instead and he did. He recalled fondly the Bothy Band years, and the fantastic music of the seventies. He has regrets that today they are not able to capitalize on their popularity, due to management decisions and legal difficulties that have plagued them since.

He is thrilled that the Bothy Band sound is as popular today as it was in the 70s, and is amazed at the vast number of young musicians who play the Bothy Band tunes at every opportunity. Paddy currently lives in America, tours extensively all over the world and his popularity with followers of Irish traditional music is as strong as ever. He has recently been to Timbuktu in Mali, Vietnam and New Zealand, and

Tokyo. He enjoys performing still and has no plans to stop playing. Undoubtedly the upbringing in Ballyfermot in the 1960s and 1970s under the careful tuition of his dad, prepared him for the life he now leads. Living in close proximity to the Fureys was another major advantage, and the times he spent performing with the Pavees was an influencial period in his musical development.. He is an iconic institution who was recognized for his talents and contribution to Irish traditional music when he was awarded the TG4 Gradam Ceol Award in the Cork Opera House in 2002. He is known and acknowledged all over the world as probably one of the greatest pipers of all time, keeping the piping flame lit by Cash and Doran alight and appreciated by a whole new Irish global family.

When Paddy Keenan is on stage, and strikes up the *Kesh Jig* or the *Ballintore Fancy*, the mood in the hall changes to excitement and appreciation of a truly great piper, carrying on the proud Traveller music tradition. Listen to either of his brothers Thomas, or Brendan on uilleann pipes and you get that same sense of something different, something exciting and extraordinary in their music.

The Keenan brothers have left an indelible stamp on Irish traditional music, just as the Dorans, Dunnes, Dohertys and Raineys before them. Lovers of Irish music all over the world owe a huge debt to this family from Ballyfermot in Dublin.

The famous Abbey Road, where the Beatles recorded

Dermie Mackin, Lissummon, Co Armagh and Paddy Keenan, Spanish Point 2008

Chapter 6: The Dunnes

Ireland's Travelling Buskers

Paddy Dunne and Freddy Williams. Hurling match Newmarket-On-Fergus, circa early 1950s. (Courtesy of Mickey Dunne and Dorothy Lange the photographer)

Experts and commentators on the Gaelic Athletic Association will tell you that there is something uniquely special about the Munster Hurling Final day in Thurles. The crowds, the colour, the friendly banter of the opposing teams' supporters form the backdrop to this eagerly awaited highlight in the province's sporting and social calendar. The scene of the Blind Dunnes entertaining the crowds with their fiddles and banjos as they made their way to and from the game, was an integral part of those great occasions for decades, They were as much a part of that scene as the supporters and the teams.

At horse racing in Galway, Munster final days in Thurles or horse fairs in Kerry, the drawing power of the Dunnes was a joy to behold. They could keep the crowds spellbound by their virtuosity on their instruments and they were an integral part of the Irish way of life. Old John Dunne was a fiddler of note and would have been known by the great Michael Coleman from Gurteen in Sligo. John Dunne played in the early days of the silent movies. According to Christy Dunne, his grandson, he had the opportunity to emigrate to America in the 1930s, but opted to stay in Ireland. Thankfully the latest generations of Dunnes continue to maintain that tradition with fervor and passion right into the 21st century. John Dunne Sr and his wife, Mary Barton, had eight children; sons Paddy, Joseph, Michael, Christy, Jack and Bernard, and daughters Mary Ann and Margaret. Some of the family had cataract problems at a time in

John Joe Dunne and his uncle Joeseph(Hanta) Dunne.
Gorey Fleadh Ceoil. circa early 1960s
(Courtesy of Mickey Dunne)

Ireland when treatment for this ailment was not readily available. They were lovingly referred to as the Blind Dunnes and, through their music, they became very popular throughout Munster. The Dunnes were originally from Co Westmeath but they eventually moved west and south and travelled extensively through Kerry, Cork, Clare Tipperary and Limerick.

"In the 1920s and 1930s, a time of great austerity in Ireland, they made their living entirely from playing music. They travelled all over the country, playing at football matches and fairs, and they often travelled into County Clare and played regularly with Johnny Doran. They busked separately, but at night-time they gathered around the campfire and played together. Johnny Doran always stood when he was busking, but my father walked through the crowd. He had what was known as a 'bottling bag' for collecting the money. It was tied

onto the coat, or, when they were playing banjos, it was hooked on to the top of the banjo. They would walk up and down through the crowd, around the four sides of the field, before, during and after the game". (Dunne, M. Limerick, 2010)

"While Christy, Mickey and Joseph were regularly recorded for radio and television, unfortunately no recording was ever made of Paddy Dunne, who was a superb fiddle player. According to Christy Dunne, the Limerick banjo player, on one memorable occasion in the 1950s when Paddy Dunne, his father, was busking outside the Cork Opera house entertaining the crowds queuing up to see the show, he was requested by the manager to play on stage. He was commissioned to stand in for the resident musician, who had taken ill, and he was paid eight pounds per week". (Dunne, C. Limerick, 2010)

As we have seen with other Traveller musician families in previous chapters, the ability to improvise while on the road was critical to their survival. Paddy Dunne reverted to using the brake cables from bicycles as a substitute for the gut strings normally used for fiddles, when he needed to replace broken fiddle strings. These improvised strings had the effect of creating a greater volume. This was a critical component in competing with the noise at football matches and fairs, thus ensuring that their music could be heard over the din. It was a trait of the Dunnes' playing that they were heard long before they could be seen. Volume was critical to their trademark, and the versatility in creating volume was a matter of survival in the competitive world of busking on the roads.

All of the Dunne family could play music. Margaret Dunne spent most of her life in a convent in Mount Merrion where she became a piano teacher. Mickey Dunne, the great Limerick piper and son of the late Paddy Dunne, recalled how his uncle, Jack Dunne, was knocked down by a car in Cork and was killed instantly. Amazingly, he had his fiddle without a case and under his coat. The fiddle was intact when his body was removed from the scene. While the Dunnes were a welcome sight all over Munster at the various events, it is important to document that not everybody welcomed them or appreciated the unique talents that they had.

Johnjo Dunne remembered vividly a Garda Hannigan who would pass by the Dunnes when they were playing outside Todd's in

Limerick and he would kick the collection box sending their money all over the Limerick streets. "Hannigan would pass by on the bus and he would see us playing on the street and he would get off the bus and come back to move us. He was a nasty piece of goods."(Dunne, J. Limerick, 2010). He also remembered a Garda McGonagle doing the same thing to his uncles when they were playing in Patrick Street, Cork. The old institutional prejudices were never too far from the surface. But the Dunnes had a simple answer for this nasty racist activity; they would get another box and start playing again.

When asked about the Traveller style of Irish traditional music, and the Traveller style of uilleann piping in particular, Mickey speaks with passion and emotion;
"There's a freedom, there is wildness, and there is a sense of pain in the Travellers' style of music. It's every emotion. When you're downtrodden all your life-and we were, make no mistake about it-it gets into your chest and it affects you. And it comes out in the playing; I can hear it in Paddy Keenan, and I can hear it in Finbar (Furey). And when I speak to Paddy Keenan about moving into the house, it was like we were brothers. He was in Ballyfermot, and I was in Limerick. These were tough times for all of us." (Dunne, M. Limerick, 2010)

Throughout the interview at the Doran Tionól in 2010, Mickey frequently returned to the theme of the attitudes to Irish Travellers, and in particular how he and his family have dealt with that. Mickey harbors some guilt about the fact that, as a young boy, he was ashamed to admit that his father was a street musician. He is now immensely proud of his Traveller heritage, and he is extremely pleased that his children share in that pride.

There was another extraordinary element to the Dunne's musicianship. They could play classical music, they were self-taught and they could play the music of Fredrick 'Fritz' Kreisler (1875-1962), the Austrian violinist and orchestral composer. The Dunnes learned from old gramophone records, playing them inside their wagon. There were few teachers, instruments were difficult to source and money was scarce, yet the Dunnes could play classical pieces of music at will. One of the last of the Dunnes to die was Joseph (Hanta) Dunne, and he busked in Limerick, near O'Mahoney's bookshop, in the 1980s. He performed classical pieces on his fiddle on the street , and he was regarded by his contemporaries as a truly superb musician.

They had busking down to a fine art. In Thurles, on Munster Final day, when the Tipperary supporters approached, the Dunne brothers played *Slievenamon*, and when the Cork contingent arrived they would break into the *Lonely Woods of Upton*.

Ireland's travelling buskers, Mickey and Christy Dunne
(Courtesy of Mickey Dunne, Limerick, 2011)

Paddy Dunne's wife, Elizabeth, was a settled person who left her comfortable lifestyle and family farm to marry the colorful Traveller musician. They established their family home in Willmount House, Janesboro in Limerick. Paddy and Lizzie Dunne had fourteen children. the boys were Stevie, Jonjo (RIP), Christy, Mickey, Jeremiah, Patrick (RIP) and Joseph, and the girls were Winnifred, Patricia, Elizabeth, Bernadette, Margaret, Cecilla and Marie. Their wide itinerary was reflected in the birth places of the children. For example Berni was born in Bantry, Margaret was born in Ballyvourney, Marie and Patrick were born in Cork, Christy was born in Tralee, Stevie was born in Caherciveen and Mickey was born in Limerick.

Mickey Dunne, uilleann piper and fiddler, is also considered by his peers to be an exceptional tin whistle player. While his father, Paddy was best known as a fiddle player, he was also a competent piper. Mickey can remember him playing *The First House in Connaught* and *The Bucks of Oranmore*, tunes closely associated with uilleann pipe players. Mickey took up the pipes when his father, Paddy, got a chanter from Finbar Furey, and a set of bag, bellows and drones from Matt Kiernan, one of the few pipe makers in Ireland at the time. Mickey now plays a full set of pipes from Cillian O'Briain, the Dingle-based uilleann pipe maker. Mickey is now an accomplished pipe maker whose pipes and reeds are much in demand.

Christy Dunne, a great banjo player with superb finger work, powerful and dynamic rhythm and an extensive repertoire of tunes, often sets the pace and tempo at his local sessions of music. Jonjo,

Left: Mickey Dunne, Limerick. (Courtesy of Mickey Dunne)

another brother, was regarded as one of the best banjo players ever. He played the instrument with the thimble, just like Johnny Keenan. Another brother, Jeremiah, was a fine accordion player and Patrick (RIP) was a wonderful fiddler. Another brother, Joseph, was an accordion player, but regretfully, gave up playing at an early age.

The next generation of the musical Dunnes is represented by Niamh Dunne, who is the lead singer and musician with Beoga , one of the best young traditional groups in Ireland, and Bríd, her sister, who is another exceptional fiddle player, classically trained , but steeped in Irish traditional music. A recent recording of Mickey and his two daughters, aptly called *Legacy*, captures the passion and intensity of the Dunnes' music, their versatility and their extensive repertoire. Stevie Dunne's son, Patrick is another superb musician and can be heard at a number of sessions in Limerick. Another niece, Kelly, plays with the Manchester Orchestra.

Mickey Dunne, tutored by his father Paddy Dunne, whom he credits with everything he knows about music, has now passed on his knowledge to another generation of young musicians, like Michael O'Connell from Co Clare, who honed his piping skills under Mickey's tutelage. Mickey and his wife, Aideen, have established a warm and welcoming environment in Caherconlish, Co Limerick, with people regularly arriving from all over the world, looking for reeds, or looking for help with tunes or repairs. He had a practice set of pipes almost completed for Daniel Fitzgerald, a 25 year-old Limerick-based Traveller related to the Doran family, but sadly Daniel was the innocent victim of a fatal shooting in December, 2009. At the time of writing, one of Daniel's cousins is interested in taking up the pipes, and Mickey is pleased that Daniel's set will be played by a member of his family.

While Mickey Dunne has breath in his body, the unique contribution of Irish Travellers to Irish traditional music will have an eloquent, passionate and principled proponent. He was deeply involved in the Nomad Project, Limerick University, which encouraged young Travellers to learn traditional music. His brother Christy, and Christy's wife, Christine, also took part in this project and Mickey was the Artist in Residence at the University in 2005, providing an insight into nuances of Irish Music for students and music lovers.

Niamh Dunne, lead singer of Beoga (Courtesy of Mickey and Aideen Dunne)

Brid Dunne, Irish traditionl and classical musician.(Courtesy of Mickey and Aideen Dunne)

Paddy Dunne was 65 when he died in 1979, just six months before Mickey got his first set of uilleann pipes. Mickey said he was a great source of encouragement, but he never forced him to play. "He would ask me if I had practiced and I would say I did. I was big into soccer and was easily distracted. He would say that 20 minutes is not enough. He would come up to the room and he would show me what to do. As a fiddle player he was one of the greatest ever, and I used to be waiting in anticipation for him to open the fiddle case and take out the instrument.

I don't go in for this concept where one musician is better than another, which to me is bullshit. Music is meant to be played and enjoyed by everyone and to an extent competition has damaged us. My Dad and my uncles played music from the heart and from the soul and they never cared or worried what anybody thought of them. Maybe that is why they were so good, they had no inhibitions. They played classical and traditional and Moore's Melodies music on the streets. The crowds loved the Dunnes playing that stuff.

I can remember my father telling me that a man came up to him in Millstreet and told him he had a Rowsome full set of pipes at home for sale. He was selling them for £50, but my dad did not have the money to buy them, but he could play the pipes; he played Johnny Doran's pipes.

They would also wheel and deal in instruments, they would sell and buy. Mickey's uncle Joe sold a great fiddle to Paddy Canny in east Clare. They would also make their own fiddles called box fiddles." (Dunne, M. Limerick, 2010)

Mickey stated that Traveller musicians have a distinct style of playing. "It just flows out of them". He compared the Travellers' approach to playing music to a native Irish speaker and a person who has been taught the Irish language. The native Irish speaker speaks without effort; and the same applies to the Traveller musicians, like Paddy Keenan, Finbar Furey, John Rooney, Johnny Purcell and Felix Doran. The music just flows out of them. Paddy Dunne would start a tune and he would have 5 or 6 reels played without a stutter, no effort whatsoever. Travellers have a unique rhythm, an expression of freedom which is distinct from non-Travellers.

Mickey regrets that today there is so much competition and so much comparing one musician to another that people are stifled, and are slow to give expression to their playing, whereas Doran, Keenan and Paddy Dunne and his uncles just played and they did not care. "Jesus, it's only a couple of tunes anyway, what's the big deal, just play the tunes and enjoy them. That's what it is about. It's only a couple of notes of music and nobody should be looking down on anybody else. Anybody who takes out an instrument, whistle, fiddle or accordion, there is great credit due to them. All of my brothers played music, but my sisters were never encouraged to play by my Dad because he associated the music with the pubs and he did not want them involved in that." (Dunne, M. Limerick, 2010)

Legacy

A number of well-known established traditional musicians readily testify to the impact of seeing the Dunne brothers perform on the streets of Limerick. Séamus Connolly, Director of Boston College for Music, stood for hours listening to the Dunne brothers playing in Limerick. Mick Moloney the Musicologist, based in New York, has stated that the first banjo player he heard was Christy Dunne. Tony McMahon has also acknowledged the enormous contribution that the Dunne family has made to Irish music.

Mickey Dunne considers the compilation of this research and publication as having major importance to the recognition of the musical contribution of Irish Travellers to Irish traditional music.

"It is so big that it cannot be quantified. If we do not have a past, as Finbar Furey said, we do not have a future. We cannot ever forget what those people have done for our Irish culture. It is huge and must never be forgotten. The Universities with their music scholarships owe a huge debt of gratitude to the Traveller musicians of Ireland and it is a source of great pride to me that I am the keeper of the flame and my family and my students have inherited something indefinable and magical. To all the Dunne Brothers of a bygone era and all the other Traveller families who preserved our culture for us and passed us the legacy. Thank You." (Dunne, M. Limerick, 2010)

The Dunne Brothers played Irish music on the streets in Limerick in the pouring rain for an Irish audience, some of whom were totally indifferent to the talent that was being played out before them. They kept our music alive, they preserved our heritage when it was not very popular to do so, and they passed a flame to the next generation that will enrich us all as a nation for generations to come.

This publication acknowledges the influences of the Dunnes on Irish traditional music. Wherever Irish music is played all over the world the influence of three generations of Traveller Dunnes should be acknowledged.

"The Legacy we leave behind will last forever"

(Mickey Dunne, February 2010)

Chapter 7: The Dohertys

Anticipation was running high in the tiny fishing village of Teelin, nestled at the foot of Slieve League, one of the most remote but spectacular places in south west Donegal. A Traveller fiddler was making his way on foot from Carrick to the village where a number of young men were waiting to take fiddle lessons from him. The March winds in 1916 were unforgiving on the narrow winding road that offered little shelter from the nearby roaring Atlantic winds.

Those who remember which one of the Doherty or McConnell families it was who helped introduce and encourage fiddle playing to Teelin have long since departed. Even in this tiny village, Teelin players would differentiate between people who played with a McConnell influence and those who played with a Doherty influence.

What is certain is that this Traveller helped established a fiddle tradition in Teelin that attracts visitors from all over the world today, producing some of Ireland's finest fiddle players. (Members of the world-famous traditional group Altan, were often to be found in the Rusty Mackerel, a friendly and inviting pub which greets the hill walkers returning from the grueling mountain hike on Slieve League, elevated by the 2,000 foot high cliffs, three times the height of County Clare's more famous Cliffs of Moher. Still high from the adrenalin of the climb, the pounding beat of Donegal music, pumped out at the breathtaking pace characteristic with the region, these visitors to this spectacular village in search of authentic Irish music, found the ideal respite. Mairéad Ní Mhaonaigh and other local musicians often entertained friends from every corner of the earth, who had been coming for years to experience the unique Teelin fiddling tradition.

The Traveller was breathing life into a living tradition, just as, at around the same time in Dublin, Mary Doran, wife of old John Doran, was about to give birth to Felix Doran, who together with his brother Johnny, would very soon join the small band of Irish Traveller musicians like the Dohertys who frequented similar remote areas of Ireland where the tradition was non-existent or under threat.

John Doherty (1900 – 1980)

John Doherty was perhaps the best-known member of that Doherty/McConnell clan who confidently traced their musical ancestry back at least three generations. Their patch was almost exclusively the south west region of Co. Donegal, where they made a comfortable living from tinkering and playing Irish traditional music. John's brother, Mickey (1894-1970), was also a well-known fiddle player, although his music was not recorded as extensively as his more famous brother.

The McConnells were related to the Gallaghers and the McSweeneys by birth and marriage and, according to a biographical note on the Comhaltas Ceoltóirí Éireann website, John often claimed that he was descended from Turloch Mac Suibhne, An Píobaire Mór, of the 18th century. (Comhaltas Ceoltóirí Éireann, 2006).

Much has been written of John's musical ancestry, and family tradition has it that his forbearers left Doe Castle on the shores of Sheep Haven at the time of the Flight of the Earls in 1607. They

were reputed to have been servants of the O'Donnell's, one of Donegal's most powerful families. John also claimed that the great piper, Turloch MacSuibhne who died in 1916 was an ancestor. (Evans, A. 1996)

"When we had the clan system, here in this country of ours, we had the O'Donnells, the O'Neills and the Maguires and so forth and so on. Each family had their own tradesmen. Not alone had they their own tradesmen, they had their storytellers; they had their poets and their men of literature. And, as I said, they had their tinsmiths and their blacksmiths too. When these families were broken up-it started off here, say after the Battle of Kinsale, after 1607, and the O'Donnells and the O'Neills like most of these tradesmen went on the road. John Doherty and his family were offsprings of these tradesmen." (*Fiddler on the Road*, Ulster TV Broadcast, 1972)

John explained that they were too "highly strung" to do manual labour, and they resorted to music and trades, such as tin smithing, for their livelihood. Like other Irish Traveller musical families, such as the Dorans and the Fureys, the Doherty's appreciated the potential complementarity of bringing useful services to rural, isolated communities by day, and the provision of music, storytelling and entertainment in the evening. Country dances in the region of Ardara, Teelin, Carrick and Glencolmcille, an area renowned for its rich fiddle tradition, resounded to the music of John's family for generations. The area eventually became famous for musicians like John Mhosey McGinley, Frank and Con Cassidy and Francie 'Dearg' and Mickey Bán O'Beirne (collectively referred to in the Kilcar area as the Deargs).

Of the nine children of Michael and Mary Doherty, at least six of them-John, Mickey, Hugh, Charlie, Mary and Simon-played fiddle, and one of the sisters was a singer. Their father Michael, and grandfather Simon (1852 -1934) and (1824 – 1899) played fiddle and bagpipes. Simon's father, Hugh Doherty (born in 1790) also played fiddle, bagpipes and uilleann pipes. Simon's brothers, Michael, played fiddle and bagpipes, and their mother, Nannie Rua McSweeney was a singer. John Doherty's mother, Mary McConnell, was also from a well-established traditional musical family. Her brothers Mickey and Alec played fiddle and bagpipes, and fiddle respectively. (Feldman, A. and O'Doherty, E.1979).

Previous Page: John Doherty

This Page: The Poisoned Glen, south west Donegal.

Together, the parents of John, Mickey and Simon Doherty were a confluence of generations of musical Irish Traveller families, steeped in the traditions of fiddle, bagpipes and uilleann pipes. The roaring Atlantic Ocean and the windswept bogs and majestic Errigal, sweeping down into the mysterious and mystical Poisoned Glen, were just some of the natural elements that breathed vitality and life into the music of this demanding and barren landscape. This amazing landscape has been woven into the very essence of these historical families of Donegal and their music for over 400 years.

The imagery of those special times in Ireland of the Doherty family arriving on horse drawn cart, with instruments, at the enchanted backdrop of Glencolmcille and Kilcar evokes a beautiful reminder of a forgotten, simpler Ireland. The Doherty family normally stayed for a month in Glencolmcille, a remote, coastal village at the heart of the Donegal Gaeltacht, providing the shops with utensils for sale, and individual homes with kitchenware and other products made from tin.

The Dohertys didn't camp by the roadside, but brought their own bed linen with them, and local families who had spare bedrooms hosted them for the full duration of their stay. This was a measure of their popularity at the time. (*Fiddler on the Road*, 1972).

John Doherty was an instinctive showman, born to entertain. He clearly appreciated the finer nuances of performance and entertainment. When asked to play a particular tune, John sparkled even as he provided an introduction, explaining the background to the tune, and taking breaks during the performance to explain a particular aspect of the piece. A good example of this is his rendering of *The Hare and the Hound*, (*Fiddler on the Road*, 1972) in which he responded to a request for a tune by standing up, giving some background to the tune, and interrupting the performance, occasionally and briefly, to draw attention to a particular piece to which he thought his audience should pay particular attention. It is clear from the expressions of the listeners that he had their full and undivided attention.

Travelling musicians of the times in Ireland had a range of skills to supplement their music, tinsmithing being but one; John had a preference for the use of the term "whitesmith", as opposed to "tinsmith" to describe his family's occupation. The Encarta

Dictionary (http://encarta.msn.com/) defines a whitesmith as 'somebody who makes or repairs objects made from white metals' or 'a metal polisher', and both these terms are accurate descriptions of the work in which Johnny and his family engaged. (A blacksmith being someone who works with heavy metals and hot coals). Working with sheets of light tin was less damaging to the fingers than blacksmithing or other arduous trades, which were deliberately avoided by the Dohertys and other Travellers dependent on their hands to make music…and money.

These Traveller minstrels made utensils for the household i.e. jugs, mugs, spoons, candleholders etc. When plastic goods replaced those items in the 1960s John was vigilant to any other opportunity to maximize the income from his brief visits to any area. In addition to making and repairing household goods, as well as providing entertainment, he often had donkeys or ponies for sale as well. Providing such essential goods and services in rurally isolated communities ensured that the Dohertys were very welcomed wherever they visited.

John Doherty pictured in the 1970s with, from left: Seán McGuire in sling (Belfast), Patsy and Martin Wilson in background (Dunkineely), Josephine Keegan (Armagh), Tommy Byrne and his son Dermot to the foreground, Joe Burke (Galway) (2705SD10)

John Doherty in Belfast with Sean McGuire, Josephine Keegan, Tommy and Dermot Byrne and Joe Burke, early 1970s (Courtesy of Josephine Keegan)

The Doherty family was extremely conscious of their reputation, and they would come together regularly in a meeting type scenario to formally review any new tunes which members had picked up on their travels. If a tune was deemed not to be of a certain standard, it would not be included in the family repertoire.

The Scottish influence on Donegal fiddle playing was very much in evidence in John's repertoire. In addition to the standard tune types played throughout Ireland, Donegal musicians had a more extensive range of tune types in their repertoire than most musicians from other counties. As well as the normal diet of reels and jigs, Donegal musicians included Highland schottisches, flings and strathspeys in their arsenal of tunes. The Scottish musical influences reflect the close economic, social and family ties between Donegal and western Scotland. Many of John's tunes also reflect the family influences of Highland pipes, which were played by many of John's ancestors. The Highlands, as a dance form, was particularly popular in south west Donegal. (Feldman, A. and O'Doherty, E.1979).

John was very impressed with, and influenced by, the music of James Scott Skinner (1843-1927). As Doherty was welcomed into houses everywhere he travelled in Donegal, he availed of the opportunity to listen to gramophone records of Skinner. He also included many of the three-minute tunes composed by Fredrick 'Fritz' Kreisler (1875-1962), the Austrian violinist and orchestral composer, in his repertoire. John could play a minimum of 700 tunes, and possibly as many as 1, 000. (Cherry, R. 2010)

When Peter Kennedy recorded John in 1953 for the recordings which Kennedy subsequently released in 1975 under the Folktrak label (the label was called Folktrak and later renamed Folktracks), Kennedy remarked that Doherty played 'almost continuously, night and day, for almost a week'. Kennedy generously advised Doherty that he should not reveal his extensive repertoire to collectors so freely, but Doherty explained that "he was anxious to record his complete repertoire of Irish, Scots and English tunes for the understanding and enjoyment of future generations."

John's brother, Mickey (1894 – 1970) was also known to have a large repertoire of tunes. When Ciarán MacMathuna recorded Mickey for RTÉ, Dr Malachy Mc Closkey from Glenties, who arranged the first meeting, recalled that Mickey played "for three to four hours", and that his repertoire included reels, jigs and a lot of strasthbeys (strathspeys) and highlands (The Rolling Wave, RTÉ, 2010).

Simon Doherty (1885-1962)

Simon Doherty was named after his paternal grandfather. His mother was in labour for a full week, and the musical fraternity did not miss the opportunity to usher in a new member of the Doherty dynasty in the appropriate fashion. Fiddlers and dancers gathered for the week around bonfires, sustaining a week of music, dance and merriment in anticipation of the big event.

Simon is the least known of the three brothers, and the least recorded, but he is remembered as a musician with an impressive repertoire of tunes. Tracks of Simon recorded by Peter Kennedy, the English folklorist, in Glenties in 1953 demonstrate powerful, strong and technically skillful fiddle playing, characteristic of the Doherty tradition. For example, his introduction to and delivery of two versions of *The Pigeon on the Gate* (Track 19) demonstrate the depth of understanding of his instrument, and its adaptability to different moods masterfully displayed in the separate nuances of the two versions. Undoubtedly, his versions of *Bonnie Kate* (Track 23) are distinguishable from John's version, and, at that level of playing, opinions on both versions merely demonstrate the preferences of the critic.

Donegal style fiddle playing was one of the last remaining unique regional styles in Ireland to be fully appreciated. As recently as the 1950s, while regional styles of Sligo, Leitrim, Clare and Kerry were being celebrated, and even mainstreamed, Donegal traditional music was being described as Scottish. John's own opinion was that "There is only a paper wall between Irish and Scottish music." (McLaughlin,

Next Page: John Doherty and John Byrne, accordion player, and brother of Dermot Byrne(Courtesy of Jimmy Gallagher and Rab Cherry)

D. (1996) *Slieve Notes; Traditional Music from Donegal.* John Doherty. Ceirníní Claddagh, 1996)

In his book, *Between the Jigs and the Reels,* (1994) Caoimhín Mac Aoidh has this to say about John Doherty's style:
"From early on John appears to have adjusted his bowing style away from his father's and his brother's Mickey's style to adopt the more dramatic staccato style and by almost totally ignoring the strong Scottish and lesser Irish dotted rhythms. This appears to have been much closer to the old style of playing in Glencolmcille which can be heard in the playing of James Byrne. It may well be that Paddy Bhillí na Ropaí whom John would have met in his youth, exerted an influence on him. At any rate through his approach, John Doherty brought fiddle playing to new heights of mastery within the Donegal context." (Mac Aoidh, C. 1994)

Donegal music is associated with fast, strong rhythms, more dependent on bowing for ornamentation than fingering. John Doherty's music reflected this regional style, but over the years he developed his own, very intricate approach to ornamentation with his left hand fingering. The Scottish influences on his repertoire were also in evidence in his style of playing. He was very inventive in imitating the sound of bagpipes drones, deploying different methods depending on the tune and the tune type.

The music of the Dohertys was eagerly anticipated wherever they travelled on their regular itinerary, and they made a lasting contribution to the preservation of Irish traditional music in County Donegal. John was 74 when he was recorded for the *John Doherty Taisce-The Celebrated Recordings.* Age didn't diminish the flair, swing, accuracy or execution of his fiddle playing. He was able to deploy a wide range of techniques to illuminate his performance and to change the mood and pathos of his delivery with ease. On *The Enniskillen Dragoons* track on *The Floating Bow,* (1996), Doherty creates a brilliant imitation of the drones of the pipes by the suppression of a string by one finger throughout the performance of the tune.

John Doherty has been recorded by many collectors and a lot of his vast repertoire is available commercially, unlike the Raineys (one cd) Johnny Doran (one cd), the blind Dunne brothers (no commercial recordings and just a few TV appearances) and Felix Doran (one commercial cd and some archived and private recordings). Non-commercial recordings include those by Alan Lomax (1915-2002), the American folklorist and collector, of Mickey, 1951, and by Peter Kennedy in 1953, the Irish Folklore Commission in 1946, recordings of John and Simon by RTÉ in 1957 and by the BBC in 1953. As Doherty was enjoying something approaching cult status up to the time of his death in 1980, a time when recording devices were plentiful and cheap, it is likely that there are many private recordings in existence. Alun Evans recorded John Doherty from 1968 to 1974, from which he compiled *The Floating Bow* CD in 1996. Evans claims that he recorded "many hours" during this period, from which he produced a generous 25 tracks of over 50 minutes of exceptional music displaying the wide range of Doherty's repertoire of reels, jigs, double jigs, slip jigs, marches, strathspeys, hornpipes, highlands and an air; a total of 36 tunes. Stories abound of Doherty's ability, in response to play a particular tune, to deliver many regional and tune type versions of the tune. Rab Cherry's claim that John Doherty knew between 700 and 1,000 tunes seems highly plausible.

In previous chapters we have identified how the social and physical landscapes influenced the music of Traveller minstrels. The bleak windswept hills of Connemara around Leenane, Letterfrack and Spiddel were evident in the Rainey's music, and with the Dorans the strong rhythmic demands of Clare Set Dancers in the 1930s and 1940s was reflected in their music.

The most striking, shared characteristic of the music of *Michael, Johnny and Simon Doherty,* in *The Flowers of Edinburgh* recordings, FTX-073 and *The Sailor's Trip* FTX-074, is the tremendous power of their music. This energy may well have been nurtured in response to the demands of playing at open air venues such as fairs and football matches where they were competing with other noises and distractions. Other Traveller musicians, notably Johnny Doran, had developed a similar style for the same reasons. However, the Dohertys, just like the Dorans, did not sacrifice technical skills in compensation for volume or power. A close examination of the Doherty brothers' playing reveals highly individual approaches to their music-making, and the well-tuned ear can quickly begin to differentiate between each of the brothers' playing.

Peter Kennedy (1922-2006) was an influencial English collector of folk songs and music in the 1950's and 1960's. He greatly appreciated the Dohertys' unique musical repertoire, and committed funds to record as much of their music as possible. He issued a number of recordings of the brothers under the Folktracks label. The company was eventually bought over by Topic Records, and the Doherty music was not rereleased. Tommy Fegan contacted Topic Records in June, 2010 and they agreed to make a copy of the Folktracks 537 recording of John and Simon Doherty. The recording consists of 24 tracks, with John and Simon playing separately, with most of the tunes introduced by each musician. It is a unique recording, due to the fact that there are few commercial or non-commercial duet recordings of any of the brothers playing together. In contrast to this, RTE did manage to record the Dohertys which included a rare recording of John and Simon playing together 'in octaves' (*The Rolling Wave*, August 20, 2010).

Folktracks Records issued a recording, made by Peter Kennedy, of Johnny and Simon Doherty-*The Sailor's Trip* in 1975 which demonstrates each player's individual style and repertoire, but sadly failed to record their duet playing. Kennedy summarized the brothers' styles, noting Johnny's repertoire of limitless tunes and Mickey's more rhythmical and danceable approach to music. His comment on Simon, of whom Kennedy says can "best be described as having more of the older country style of Irish fiddle-playing" conceals more of the author's opinion of Simon than it reveals. (http:// Folktracks -archive.org/menus/cassprogs/273.htm)

The Ulster Television programme on the life and music of John Doherty, entitled, Fiddler on the Road, claimed that Johnny was the "last of a family of four." However, the family tree produced in the *Northern Fiddler* (Feldman, A. O'Doherty, E. (1979), lists nine children born to Mickey Mór Doherty and Mary MacConnell.

Caoimhin Mac Aoidh, one of the leading authorities on the Dohertys, eloquently and vividly recalled John Doherty's final days;
"On a Monday morning in late January, 1980 I called in to see him and we parted with him thundering out *The Black Fanad Mare* with the energy of a teenager. He died peacefully, the following Thursday. On the following freezing Saturday he was buried in Fintown Cemetery. The mass, which was especially broadcast live on Radió na Gaeltachta sent out the message that one of the greatest traditional

musicians and possessors of folklore had passed on. The bitterly icy conditions made travelling impossible for the great numbers who wished to pay their respects at his funeral. A small group that gathered in the Welcome Inn pub outside Fintown paid suitable compliment to John. After a drink, a single fiddle was produced and given to Vincent Campbell. He hammered out a reel in honour of John then spotted another player to whom he handed the instrument. He played a tune then passed on the fiddle. After a while it was discovered that the only ones in the house who could not play were the barman and the three women present. Eventually fiddles appeared from under coats, beneath seats, the backs of cars and a massive musical testimony to one of the giants of Irish music ensued." (*Between the Jigs and the Reels*, Drumlin Publications, 1994, pp. 239-240).

Mickey Doherty (Courtesy, National Folklore Collection, UCD)

Legacy

John Doherty along with his brothers and uncles, made a significant contribution to the Donegal fiddle playing tradition. The Dohertys were related to three other Traveller musician families-the McSweeneys, the McConnells and the Gallaghers. They were also related to the O'Rourke and the McGinley Traveller families who also had musical branches. Together, these families brought Irish traditional music to isolated communities in Donegal over at least five generations, spanning three centuries.

John Doherty was the youngest family member of the Doherty family who played music, and much more material is available on his music, including commercial and private recordings, newspaper articles and television and radio interviews, than exists for any other members of the family. This has helped ensure that his legacy will sustain when the talents and achievements of other members of the family may diminish in time.

The Donegal style of fiddle playing has impacted hugely over the years on the development of Irish traditional music, and some of the top music groups in Ireland have had a Donegal influence in their make up.

The original line-up of the Bothy Band included Donegal fiddle player Tommy Peoples. His music is unmistakably of his own county, and we have demonstrated in this chapter how the Dohertys and their extended musical Traveller families were instrumental in helping define Donegal's energetic and pulsating sound. This became a vital ingredient for the Bothy Band. Other key components of that sound included two other Donegal musicians, Tríona Ní Dhomhnaill, and her brother Mícheál Ó Domhnaill. The group that was the precursor to the formation of the Bothy Band was Seachtar, whose line-up closely resembled that of the Bothy Band, with the exception of Paddy Glackin, who was Seachtar's fiddle player. Paddy's fiddle style is strongly reminiscent of the Donegal style, partly attributable to the influence of his father, Tom, who was born and reared in west Donegal. Paddy readily acknowledges Doherty's influence on his playing. Glackin eventually left Seachtar to pursue a professional career in broadcasting, and Tommy Peoples took his place in the new line-up which renamed itself the Bothy Band. A critical component of the emergence of the band that made a major contribution to the popularity of Irish traditional music from the mid 1970's on can be traced back to County Donegal and to John Doherty in particular. The Dohertys from Donegal share pride of place with Coleman, Morrison, Doran and Tuohy as major influences on the development of Irish traditional music in the 20th century.

The Donegal Democrat hinted at Doherty's links to nobility when it announced his death with the following headline "John Doherty-Prince among traditional fiddlers-is dead." (*Donegal Democrat*, 1st. February, 1980).

Next Page; Mickey Mór Doherty and sons l-r John, Mickey Mór, Mickey Doherty, John Doherty (Courtesy of Jimmy Gallagher and Rab Cherry)

Chapter 8: The Raineys

The CD, *The Raineys* (Pavee Point, Dublin, 2007), a recording of Paddy 'Big' Rainey, his brother Stephen 'Spare Parts' Rainey, and Paddy's wife Bridget 'Biddy' Rainey, brought the music of this Traveller family to a wide audience when it was released in 2007. Prior to this, very little information was available about the family, and their music was virtually unknown, except by those few people still alive who remembered them playing on their travels throughout Co Galway from the 1930s to the late 1950s. Martin Rochford (1916-2000), fiddle player and piper from County Clare, recalled listening to Tony Rainey playing the uilleann pipes in O'Connell Square, Ennis on a summer's evening in 1935. (Rochford, M. Co Clare, 1988) Rochford was very impressed with Rainey's command of the pipes, and his regulator playing in particular. He remembered him playing *The Heathery Breeze* so well that a member of the crowd from Kilmaley, Co Clare, asked him to repeat the tune. Rochford thought that they "came from Carlow, or over that part of the country.", and that "he had four or five brothers, all of whom were pipers." An editorial note to this article suggests that Tony Rainey may be one of the Raineys referred to in *An Píobaire*, Issue 2 Volume 20, who are the subject of this chapter.

Stephen Rainey is one of the earliest musicians of that name associated with uilleann pipe playing in County Galway. Uilleann

The Raineys. (CD cover picture, courtesy of Pavee Point, Dublin))

piper Andy Conroy suggested Stephen, and his son Michael, were amongst the last of the genuine old-time pipers after the death of John Reilly, the blind piper from Dunmore, Co Galway in 1927 (Conroy, A. *An Píobaire*, Issue 2 Volume 20, 1994)

Michael Rainey, and his father Stephen, are mentioned in the O'Cassaide papers as being from Ballinasloe, Co Galway, although Conroy suggested they were from Tuam. (*An Píobaire*, 1994). Michael Walsh (1914-1995) was born in Headford, Co Galway and emigrated to America in 1936. Walsh is reported by Bill Ochs as being impressed by one of the Raineys who was a piper and whose family often passed through Headford. (Ochs, B. 1995). As many of those interviewed for Ita Kane's 2001 radio documentary for Connemara Community Radio, *The Raineys of the Road* located Paddy and Stephen Rainey travelling in the Headford area in the 1950s, the likelihood is that these are members of the same family group. In addition, Kane refers to Paddy and Stephen Rainey as being nephews of Stephen Rainey, the uilleann piper mentioned above by Andy Conroy.

Paddy Rainey, known as 'Big Rainey', and his brother Stephen, known as 'Spare Parts', travelled through Connemara playing Irish traditional music on fiddles. Paddy's wife, Biddy, who was from Northern Ireland, was a singer, contributing to the versatility and popularity of their performances.

Mary Lynat from Liskevey, near Tuam, remembers when she was a young child hearing about the Raineys, who like many others, had been forced off their land during the land troubles;

"They had a farm of land up in Liskevey but the landlords or whoever evicted them and they stayed around Liskevey for a while in a barn, and then they went on the road."(Lynat, M. 2001)
Mickey Doherty from Caloburn, near Tuam, remembers his father talking about the Raineys, supporting the view that Paddy and Stephen are from the same family group as the five Rainey brothers who were uilleann pipers;

"Old Rainey I heard of and his wife- I don't know their names only

I knew him as Old Rainey -I didn't know him now, he was before my time, but I heard my father talk about them. He played the pipes, he was a musician. He stayed in the house in the village beside us, in Bunowen. He played there every night around the village. There were seven or eight houses in the village, and they all let in the young lads and lasses every night of the week dancing. And he went from house to house. Came back again to(inaudible) and slept there." (Doherty, M. *Raineys of the Road*, 2001)

Doherty was able to name the five brothers-Stephen, Mike, Pat, Anthony and Jack, and the instruments they played. The Steven and Pat to whom he refers are most likely 'Spare Parts' and 'Big Rainey', who Professor Tony Rowland recorded in Letterfrack in 1956.

"During the day then, himself (Old Rainey) and the wife would go off and beg, I suppose, and get a few things around the area. Then in the summertime they would go off about the country. They probably had a donkey and cart. Seemingly, though, they had five sons, who all had gone their own way at this time now. Anthony who played the flute and Stephen who played the flute as well, Mike played the pipes; Pat played the fiddle, and Jack played the tin whistle. Those were their five sons. I knew all those five sons personally." (Doherty, M. 2001)

The Mike referred to here by Doherty is more than likely to be the uilleann piper Andy Conroy referred to above. This is further evidence to support the view that Spare Parts' and 'Big Rainey'are grandsons of Michael Rainey, one of the last of the old style pipers left after the death of John Reilly in 1927.They were frequent visitors to the home of Sarah and Rita Keane, the famous singers from Caherlistrane. They had fond memories of Stephen and his wife Alice;

"They'd come over in the summertime from Letterfrack. They used to walk it when they came. I don't know how long it took them; maybe a day and a half or so. But they'd arrive anyway,(and from Cornamona and Clonbur, voices in background) and they would camp up the road there, and Stephen would go around playing the timber flute, and she would sing. She was a lovely singer. She was the first woman I ever heard singing *The Green Fields of Derry. The High Walls of Derry*, they call it now. She was a gifted singer; a lovely little

smart woman, a very educated woman. She was a northerner, from Northern Ireland. She had a northern accent at that time, which we used to think was very strange. And she had her own little quiver, like the northerners had, and she was able to step dance; dance a jig, reel or hornpipe, in here on the floor. My parents were gone to Tuam one day, and the back door and the front door were open, which is not normal any more. And she was dancing in the middle of the floor, from one door to the other. And we had no work done at all when they came home from Tuam. They were very vexed about it. We waited all day, watching her dancing and singing, and her husband playing. We didn't do a stroke of work." (Keane, S & R. *Raineys of the Road*, 2001)

Gabriel O'Sullivan, also known as The Gabe, was a well-known flute player who grew up with the Raineys in Headford, eventually settling in London in 1940. In his interview with Ita Kane for *The Raineys of the Road*, he conveys the esteem in which the travelling family was held by his father, neighbours and community at that time;
"I was a young lad then, just six years of age and I had the measles. I was upstairs in the bed, and it was a bit lonesome there, with no one coming near me. And I could hear the loveliest of music below in the kitchen. And I jumped out of bed with the pyjamas on me and went down to the door, but I couldn't open the latch on the door; it was too high. I knocked on it, and my father came out. And he said, 'Where are you going?' And I said, 'I heard the most beautiful music, out here.' And he said, 'Come on in.'

And old Pat Rainey was playing there, and my father and he were having a few lovely whiskeys for themselves. And he said, 'This is the great Pat Rainey, the great fiddle player.' And so I stuck out my hand. 'How are you Pat?' said I. 'No, he (Gabriel's father) said, 'How are you, Mr Rainey?' Because that was the kind of man he was, and Rainey put the fiddle into my hand, and he said, 'You will be a fiddle player yet, but it will break your heart like it has broken all our hearts.' So he said, 'Give it back to me.' And he played a lovely reel called *The Mullingar Races*."

Mike played the pipes at fairs and things like that. And the pipes were a bit awkward to stand up, and he had a camog stick, he'd stick this under the leg for the chanter, you see. Mike that played the bagpipes was married. And he would come with the wife with him and the big

ginnet and cart, and a tent at the side of the road. It was even hard for the people to give them something. They were happy, and they went from house to house, and the people gave them whatever they could give them, a drop of milk, a grain of flour, maybe or anything that was going on that time. And when they went to the fair playing their different instruments they would get a few pence or coppers and that amounted to quite a few pounds."(Sullivan, G. *Raineys of the Road*. 2001.)

Another, unidentified, interviewee on *The Raineys of the Road* programme recalled how Pat and Biddy often camped near their home in Liskevey. His father asked him to call down to the Rainey's camp and ask Pat or Biddy to call to the house that evening "because there are lots of hard boiled eggs and loaves and everything left over, and let them come up with a bag. And tell Pat Rainey that I have two pairs of shoes for him and two pairs of old trousers." When the young messenger arrived at the tent, he heard music coming from inside;
"And the next thing I heard this music coming out from under that cab. I don't know if there was two fiddles, and aul Pat playing the tinkeen melodeon, or was it Paidin himself and auld Pat playing the tinkeen melodeon. But I never heard nicer. They played *Miss McLeod's* reel and *The Swallow's Tail*." (Unknown interviewee, *Raineys of the Road*, 2001)

Ita Kane's interview with Mary Mullen, from Moylough, raises further questions about the family members, their names and the instruments they played. Mary Mullen's family were the owners of the local shop, which was frequented by the Rainey family. She and her friends were often delayed on their way home from school as they lingered at the Rainey's camp listening to their music. Recalling how Biddy reported the contents of her day's begging to her husband, Mary Mullen remembers Biddy saying, 'Look at that, Mickey'. The only Rainey by the name of Mickey, or Michael, so far identified in this research, other than Michael, father of Steven, is one of the five sons of Stephen Rainey, Mickey Rainey, who played uilleann pipes. She goes on to observe that their son Paddy died in England and that "he played the fiddle with two fingers only. First and second, he

Previous Page, Margaret Rainey holding a picture of her father Big Pat Rainey, Galway 2010.(Courtesy of Tommy Fegan)

never used the others but still played his reels."(Mullen, M. 2001)

Professor Tony Knowland , the English folklorist who recorded Paddy 'Big' Rainey and Stephen ' Spare Parts' Rainey in Letterfrack in 1956, did not mention in his sleeve notes to the CD, or in his interviews with Ita Kane, that Paddy Rainey only played with two fingers. This suggests that the Paddy Rainey who played with two fingers was the son of Mickey Rainey, who was a brother of Pat 'Big' Rainey and Stephen 'Spare Parts' Rainey. This deduction is further supported by the observation by Mary Mullen that she enjoyed listening to "young John especially playing the fiddle." (Mullen, M. 2001). There have been no known previous references to a John Rainey in this family group.

Desmond O'Haloran, a singer and musician from Innisbofin, recalled the lasting impression Paddy and Stephen had on him as a teenager in Cleggan, and, over 30 years later in England, how he instantly recognised the Rainey sound;

"I remember fishing in Innisbofin, when I was around 17. And one bad night we went ashore and went to Oliver's and I remember Paddy Rainey playing there very well, and the wife singing. And then when I went to London years after, and I was years in London. I then went to Leeds for two years to live. And then went into this pub in Leeds called the Regent, and I said to one of the people that was with me, I said "I think I heard that kind of music before you know." And after 30 odd years, I went in the door and I asked somebody who was playing and they said, "It's John Rainey" and it was exactly the same kind of music. I'm not sure if John is still alive here. I was in his house a few times in Leeds."(O'Halloran, D. 2001)

Tom Healey was a singer and songwriter from Cleggan. In a song that he wrote about them, he made reference to Spare Part's versatility in maintaining the fiddles;

"Big Rainey, his fiddle with a hole in it,
And carpet hairs for strings and the bow
Jimmy Mullen said he could not knock a note of it."
(Healey, T. 2001)

Jimmy Mullen, referred to in Healey's song, recalled one occasion when he witnessed Big Rainey fixing his fiddle; "He had no hair in the bow, but he had black thread-spool thread- and he stretched it, and played music and put resin on it, and when I tried to play I failed; he was a genius." (Mullen, J. 2001)

Professor Tony Knowland was also amazed at the state of Paddy's fiddle, and the unorthodox methods he used to maintain it; "It was the most extraordinary instrument I have ever seen in my life. There was hardly a square inch of varnish on it. There was a gaping hole in the belly of it. The bow which he had was treaded with carpet tread, and it was fastened at the heal through with a cotton bobbin and a nail." (Knowland, T. Professor. 2001)

Margaret Rainey, a daughter of Pat and Bridget, now lives in a house on the Headford Road, Galway. She provided a rare, firsthand account of busking with her uncle, Stephen 'Spare Parts, and her mother, to Ita Kane in 2001;

"I would go with my uncle; sometimes my mother would come with us and we had bikes, we'd cycle bikes. We would just walk in the gates, stand at the door, and my uncle would play, and two seconds later the door would be opened, and the people would say, "Come on in." We might be half an hour in that house, playing and then we'd be given some money, and we'd go on to the next house and do the same thing, and my father would go down then to Leenane. He'd always say, "As long as I have the price of the hatch." That meant it was price of the first drink, after that he was fine. He was able to get the rest from there on. Then my mother would go down in the evening, about five o'clock and she would join my father, and they would play and sing for the rest of the night on, and she would go around then, with the knobber, as we called it. 'Twas a bag that we made out of pieces of material, and put a bit of wire in it and the top of that was open(about that width) and she would hold it and the people would just throw money into it."(Rainey, M. 2001)

A perspective of how the music and the musicians were received during one of these house calls was provided by Charlie O'Malley, a musician from Renvyle, when he recounted a visit from the Raineys while he, his father and neighbours were taking a break from hay-making;
"It was a weekday, and we were making a rick of hay, gathering in the hay with a horse and cart (with) a couple of neighbours there, like Stephen Kane and Patrick O'Malley, two of my friends and neighbours, and we were having tea around three o'clock in the afternoon and this beautiful music just started outside the door, and I tell you, to the day I go to the grave, I don't think I will hear anything as sweet or as nice, because it was unusual to hear any strange music coming around the neighbourhood. Who was standing outside the door but Pat Rainey, and, good God, he came in. My mother answered the door and told him to come in and said 'Céad mile fáilte' because she was an Irish speaker, and brought Pat in and his wife. They came in first, and my old dad got up and shook hands and says that we will have to have some tea first. "Well, Missus," he (Pat Rainey) said, "While you're making a pot of tea, I'll play you a couple of tunes." and he started off anyway, and he played the *Sligo Maid* and *The Sally Gardens. The Sally Gardens* was a new reel at the time, and everyone wanted to have it, and he put his own version on it." (O'Mallley, C. 2001)

Biddy Rainey undoubtedly added to the popularity of the Raineys as they travelled throughout Connemara earning a living from their music. While their music was well received in an area where traditional Irish dance music was appreciated, the popular song tradition of Connemara ensured that Biddy's contribution was also well received. The owner of the pub in Letterfrack in which the recording of the Raineys was made, told Knowland that 'she was one of the best Irish ballad singers i had ever heard'. (Professor Tony Knowland, 2001).From the only recording available, *The Rainey's* CD, we know that Biddy's repertoire was not confined to old traditional songs. Tom Munnelly recognised that her choice of songs was very much influenced by songs that had a popular appeal at that time;

"And the song is very much influenced by popular waltzing, and particular singers like Bridie Gallagher, who was extremely popular at the time. But in the case of her singing, to me, and I have been working with Traveller singers for a long, long time, I wouldn't have picked her out as a Traveller singer straight away. But she is a singer, and she is a show woman. But if you are busking, you have to please the people who are listening to you, and this is the sort of singing they want to hear, so this was the sort of singing she was performing. Herself and her husband are obviously extremely well used to performing together. He is picking up on the nuances of her singing,

The Pat Rainey Song, by Fergus Russell, 2007

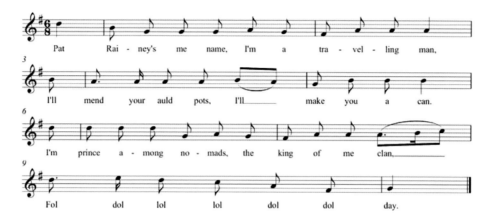

Pat Rai - ney's me name, I'm a tra - vel - ling man,
I'll mend your auld pots, I'll____ make you a can.
I'm prince a - mong no - mads, the king of me clan,____
Fol dol lol lol dol dol day.

1.
Pat Rainey's me name I'm a travelling man
I'll mend your auld pots, I'll make you a can
I'm prince among nomads, the king of me clan
Fol dol lol lol dol dol day

2.
I travel the roads with me ass and me dog
There's game in the fields, there's turf in the bog
I sing like a lark as along we do jog.
Fol dol lol lol dol dol day

3.
I camps by the river I catches a fish
I always have plenty to put in me dish
Me brogues I can mend and me clothes I can
    stitch
Fol dol lol lol dol dol day

4.
I gathers me pipes, I heads for the town
I finds a good pitch and I sets meself down
I squeeze on the bellows; the throng gather
    round
Fol dol lol lol dol dol day

5.
I plays "Misses McCloud" and "The Wind in the
    Gap"
It pleases the crowd, they dance and they clap
And many bright shillings they put in my cap
Fol dol lol lol dol dol day

6.
I'm fond of a glass for I think it no crime
I sit in the Shebeen 'mid comrades sublime
I'll dance til the dawn cos I'm not slave to time
Fol dol lol lol dol dol day

7.
The housewife each night she slips down from
    the farm
Her husband is cold but I am quite warm
And here in me tent, sure she'll come to no harm
Fol dol lol lol dol dol day

8.
When winter comes on, for fear of the damp
I'll whistle me dog, down the road we will tramp
And the housewife will sigh, when she sees
    we've broke camp
Fol dol lol lol dol dol day

9.
When springtime it blossoms, I'll pass by this
    way
I'll boil up me billy, I'll make me some tay
And I'll check if the *buffer* has one on the way
Fol dol lol lol dol dol day

10.
Pat Rainey's me name I'm a travelling man
I can mend your auld pots, I can make you a can
I'm prince among nomads, the king of me clan
Fol dol lol lol dol dol day

and likewise she is fitting her singing very well into his fiddle playing. Whereas Traveller singing unaccompanied uses a certain amount of what is called port mental-sliding from note to note-it's a style or decoration that is common with Travellers. But if you were singing to fit in with accompaniment, obviously this dictates the form in which you sing, so it will iron out accompaniment. So it is difficult to tell what she would have been like singing on her own. Certainly it would have been interesting to hear her." (Tom Munnelly, 2001)

As well as singing songs that were popular at the time, such as *Kitty Daly*, and songs she was learning from the radio, Biddy also sang Irish rebel songs. Her daughter Margaret recalled that 'if she was singing, then one or two people would stand at the door to protect the man of the pub. If the Guards came they could stop her from singing and get her to change over to something else.'(Rainey, M.2001)

Biddy, Paddy and Stephen were frequently busking and performing in the public houses in Connemara during the 1940s and 1950s, a period during which it was unusual for women to attend such establishments. Phil Coyne, from Mullaglass, Renvyle, remembered people commenting on this fact, but he also recalled that she was a very good singer and was much appreciated." (Coyne, P. 2001).

Professor Tony Knowland's account of how he made the famous, and only, recording of the Raineys reveals something of Paddy Rainey's sense of dignity;

"These chaps, being professional, weren't at all fazed by the presence of a microphone, and I had a big Grundig microphone which we put on the bar but they, obviously being professional, were quite happy to play in public and weren't fazed. So they played and of course we had to celebrate the playing with a pint. And then, 'Can we play it back?' So we played it back, and we had to celebrate that with another pint and this went on until about six o'clock in the evening, recording and playing back and celebrating on each occasion until eventually I said that I would have to go back home now. And then I thought to myself, 'Well, look here, these chaps are living out of a horse and cart and making a little bit of money by passing the hat around at the end of the session. I surely must make some gesture to them. So I did.
I took out a ten shilling note, which in those days was quite a lot of money, bearing in mind that the price of Guinness for a pint was ten old (pence) , which is about £2.50 now. Nobody drank anything else but Guinness in those days because whiskey and spirits were too expensive. So I took out this ten shilling note and went to give it to Big Rainey, but he seized my hand and he wouldn't take it. 'You have a whiskey,' he said. He was not going to be condescended to by some middle-class English gentleman. But eventually towards the end of the evening, I did manage to slip the ten shilling note into the top pocket of his jacket, thinking, these chaps deserve every penny of it."(Knowland, T. Professor. 2001)

Fiddle Style

The Rainey's style of fiddle playing is laid-back and easy-going. No attempt is made to inject the level of ornamentation that was, and continues to be, prevalent in Irish traditional fiddle playing. Pat, in particular, made copious use of the droning technique in which additional strings are played simultaneous to the melody line. While it is reminiscent of techniques used in County Donegal, the structure, rhythm and pace of the music is unlike any of the north western counties such as Sligo, Leitrim or Donegal, noted for their highly distinctive fiddle styles. John Faulkner, in his interview for the *Raineys of the Road* radio programme, speculated that, due to the absence of ornamentation which was a hallmark of Michael Coleman and James Morrison's recordings, brought back from America in the 1930s and 1940s, the Rainey's music may have reflected the style of music played in Ireland prior to the period of mass exodus in the 19th century. He cites the similarities with Appalachian old-style fiddling playing, which emerged in America in the 18th and 19th centuries. While the Raineys' music lacks the ornamentation and variation which Johnny and Felix Doran embedded in their interpretation of tunes, there is no mistaking the similar sense of adventure and wildness shared by these two Traveller families, one from the East Coast and one from the West Coast of Ireland.

The Legacy

Other Irish Traveller families who played Irish traditional music, in Ireland and England, have not heard of or met Travellers from the family group. Unlike the Fureys, Dorans, Dunnes and Keenans, who continue to maintain their family musical traditions, the Raineys do not appear to have maintained that rich, musical heritage in the current generation. Nor is there any evidence that musicians outside the family group incorporated the Rainey style into their interpretation of Irish traditional music. Yet musicians, such as Martin Rochford and Andy Conroy, were very impressed with the Raineys, and in the absence of any concrete evidence, it is impossible to isolate and link the influence of the Raineys to current styles of Irish traditional music. But Dublin based singer, Fergus Russell, was sufficiently moved by the music he heard at the launch of *The Raineys* CD in 2007, that he composed a song in praise of Paddy 'Big' Rainey. Russell awoke the morning after the launch of the CD in Dublin, and *The Pat Rainey Song* music and lyrics had completely formed in his mind in his sleep.

Paddy Rainey eventually got tired of the nomadic lifestyle, and, according to his daughter Margaret, he was keen to create a better life for his children. A local authority councillor in Carrondonna in Galway had arranged a house for them, but the arrangement was never realised. When Pat Rainey heard that he was offered the house in preference to a woman with young children, he insisted that her need was greater, and rejected the offer in her favour. With no other accommodation available to him, he moved reluctantly to Manchester with Steven and their children. The brothers continued to play music together in their respective houses, and so far there is no evidence that they joined in with the Irish traditional music scene in Manchester, which was thriving there in the late 1950s. Felix Doran's son, Mikey, has no knowledge of hearing of the Raineys in the Manchester area, where they lived most of their lives. (Doran, M. 2010). Stephen took a job with the local county council. He was forced, due to ill health, into early retirement and died shortly afterwards. Paddy died after falling down the stairs in his home. At the time of the recording of the radio programme, in 2001, Margaret was the only member of the family living in Ireland, and Biddy was still in Manchester. She stopped singing when Paddy died.

Margaret feels that her father was not happy in Manchester, and that he missed the open spaces of Connemara, especially Lennane, Letterfrack and Cleggan.

'I think his spirit is still out there.'

(Margaret Rainey, The Raineys of the Road)

Stokes wedding in Derry outside Bar
(Courtesy of Navan Travellers Workshop)

Chapter 9: The Pecker Dunne

The Pecker Dunne (1932-)

"I never met Bob Dylan,
But I sang with Pecker Dunne
And when we drank Lough Erin dry
We went looking for Lough Dan"
(Christy Moore, Ceol na bhFánaith,
TG4, 2005))

Pádraig Dunne was born in Castlebar, Co Mayo in 1952. "We were living on the side of the road in New Ross and I used to ride horses for a Major Peckard - they called me 'Major Peckard' after that and then shortened it to 'Pecker'." His father, Stephen Dunne, was born in Loughrea, Co Galway and his parents and grandparents were Travellers musicians. Pecker's mother, Annie Byrne, was from a settled family in Wexford. Both of Pecker's parents played music to raise income for their young family of five children; Nellie, Stephen, Mary-Anne, Annie and Pecker. Pecker's earliest memories of childhood included travelling from their camp site into the nearest town or village on horse and pony with his father to busk. His father combined playing music for a living with buying and selling horses and ponies. Both activities complimented their nomadic lifestyle. Pecker's father instilled in him the value of music as a source of income and he began teaching Pecker at an early age. Pecker also received tuition from his uncle Briany Dunne. Pecker, his father and his uncle later travelled on bicycles from their camp to the local towns and villages.

When Pecker and his siblings reached school-going age, the family confined their travels to Co Wexford, and the children were educated at St Bridget's National School. There he met other young people from the Traveller community, many of whom were from Travellers musicians' families, such as the Connors and the Dunnes. His recollections of the Traveller children being put together on one side of the classroom from the other children was one of his earliest introductions to prejudice and discrimination practised against Travellers in Ireland. It was the theme that would feature in his song writing in years to come, as he articulated that exclusion in songs such as *The Travelling People* and others.

Pecker had his first introduction to alcohol on the day he made his Confirmation, aged 12. He got drunk on that occasion, but recalls enjoying the feeling; "This is good. I like this."(*Parley-Poet and Chanter*, Dunne, P.2004, p 12) Pecker left school shortly after, still aged 12, to go travelling full-time.

Pecker's father introduced him to the fiddle and encouraged him to adopt music as his principal source of livelihood. "There you go, there is your living. If you don't play it, you will go hungry. It's that simple." (*Parley-Poet and Chanter*, Dunne, 2004, p 12) Eventually, Pecker moved from playing fiddle to banjo, much to his father's regret. When Pecker's father died, in the mid-1950s, Pecker stopped playing the fiddle for over 15 years. On a visit to his home in Killimer, Co Clare, in July, 2010, to record him playing, we noticed that, despite his ill health, he remained versatile on both instruments. However, the banjo appeared to be more physically demanding of him, and on this and a subsequent visit in August, 2010, Pecker's preference for the convenience of the fiddle was obvious.

Pecker's grandfather played the fiddle, and his grandmother played the melodeon. His grandfather was from Kilbeggan, Co Meath, and was descended from a long line of fiddle players. His grandmother, Mary Ann Rowes, was a tightrope walker with a travelling circus. She was also an accomplished melodeon player, despite the fact that she was deaf. His grandmother often busked at St Bridget's National School, sometimes calling to take the young Pecker out of the class early and buy him sweets with some of her earnings. She carried her melodeon hidden inside her shawl. When she played duet with Pecker's grandfather, she would catch hold of his fiddle to ensure that she could pick up the correct rhythm, which was not available to her, due to her deafness.

Next Page: Pecker Dunne at home in Killimer (Courtesy of Tommy Fegan)

Pecker's father and mother moved into their first house in the New Street, in Crumlin, Dublin when he and his sisters were young. His father was anxious that they got an education. Later the family moved to England when one of Pecker's sisters got married and moved there. Like his father, Pecker worked in various labouring jobs by day, and supplemented his income by playing music in bars at night. He worked in a rubber factory in Bury, in a gasworks in Stoke, and in the train station in Birmingham.

In addition to the two occasions when he lived and worked in England, Pecker also spent two months travelling in Australia. He went to Australia when he was 17, and the wide open spaces of that continent appealed to his nomadic instincts. He stayed with various aboriginal nomadic tribes on a number of locations, and he claimed that their favourite song of his was *Whiskey in the Jar*.

After his father died in the mid-1950s, Pecker returned to Dublin, teamed up with a musician called George Nash, and secured a regular booking in the Old Shelling bar. This proved to be a turning point in his musical career, and from then on, his sole economic activity was singing and playing music. In the early 1960s, he was invited to tour with The Dubliners folk group in America, then one of the most popular Irish bands in the vanguard of the Irish folk and traditional revival. Pecker shared a lot of characteristics and interests with Dubliner Luke Kelly; they both had very distinctive heads of thick curly hair, they both preferred songs with very strong social content and messages, they had very distinctive voices and they both accompanied themselves on banjo. Both of them also spent time living in England by day and learning and honing their music and songs in clubs and bars by night.

Pecker never missed an opportunity to give voice to the injustices suffered by Irish Travellers. Many of his compositions, such as The Last of *The Travelling People* and *Wexford Town*, were melodic, assertive and sensitive testimonies to the Irish Traveller lifestyle, and his pride in this role was evident in his composition, delivery and passion;

With my banjo and fiddle I'll ya a song,
I'll sing to all people who do me no wrong,
But if others despise me I'll just move along,

Pecker Dunne at home in Killimer, Co Clare with Tommy
Fegan (pipes) (Courtesy of Oliver O'Connell)

I know I find friends in the morning,
(*The Last of the Travelling People*, Dunne, P. page 117)

He avoided trivia in his compositions, and addressed directly the issues of the day which were not debated openly in Irish society; discrimination, emigration, alcoholism and poverty. His closeness to nature, his love of the countryside and his acute observation enabled him to identify and articulate many current issues of the day.

I am a little rabbit and I cannot see the feed
For both my eyes are rotted out for the sake of human greed
(*The Last of the Travelling People*, Dunne, P. page 118)

Another aspect of Irish Travellers' culture of which Pecker was extremely proud was the language spoken by Travellers in Ireland, Cant. He makes liberal use of Cant words throughout his book, Parley-Poet and Chanter. All of the chapter headings and subheadings are accompanied by translations for words and phrases. For example, Mozying (moving) into the casi (house), the cris nudes (old people) passing on. (p. 22)

Legacy.

Pecker has passed on to his children the musical legacy he inherited from his parents and former generations of Dunnes who playedIrish traditional music as a major source of income. His son Tommy plays uilleann pipes, Stephen plays the banjo, fiddle and pipes, his daughter Sarah plays concertina and fiddle and his wife Madeleine plays accordion.

In addition to his considerable contribution to maintaining the ballad tradition of street busking at major events throughout almost every county in Ireland, and regular appearances in England and America, many of his own compositions have been assimilated and adopted into the tradition. Most notable of these is *Sullivan's John*, a song he composed when he was 12 years of age.

"O Sullivan's John to the roads you have gone, far away from your native home
You've gone with a tinker's daughter, along the roads to roam,
O Sullivan's John you wont stick it long, till your belly will soon go slack
You'll be out on the road with a mighty load, and your toolbox on your back"
(*Sullivan's John*, Pecker Dunne)

Pecker bows using his knees, at home with Madeline Dunne in Killimer, Co Clare, 2010 (Courtesy of Tommy Fegan)

Chapter 10: John Rooney

John Rooney, Manchester, 2009 (Courtesy of Tommy Fegan)

It was late February 2000, in Wicklow town and as we walked into the Wicklow Hotel at 7pm in the evening, we were greeted by a wall of music that emanated from the lounge bar situated on the ground floor. The music was wild and the sense the excitement as you entered the room was almost tangible. Nine uilleann pipers were in full flow, and centre stage in that group was a well built, strong-looking individual who was very much in charge of this session. He stood out from the rest of the group which consisted of Paddy Keenan, Mickey Dunne Michael McGoldrick, John McSherry and a host of other pipers. This was John Rooney, son-in-law of the great Felix Doran and he was tapping out Doran's tunes to an appreciative audience. He was also barking out instructions to some of the younger pipers and it was an extraordinary experience to watch him in action.

The first Johnny Doran Piping Tionól was being held in the Wicklow Hotel and the extended Doran, Purcell and Rooney families had arrived in Wicklow for the event.

John Rooney, who could be classified as the patriarch of the Doran/Cash piping dynasty, was born in Crossmaglen, Co Armagh in 1952 to Big Johnny Rooney and Nan Delaney, daughter of Felix Doran, John is married to Bridgie Doran.

John's father played the old Clarke tin whistle, and he was a very close friend of Felix Doran, the piping icon of the time. In 1967 they went to the Fleadh in Clones, Co Monaghan and John was mesmerized at the sight of Felix tuning the pipes at an informal gathering of musicians and music lovers on the main street. "And that was it", exclaimed John, as he committed himself there and then to a lifetime of carrying on the proud Doran tradition. John's father asked Felix to let young John try on his pipes. He played *The Boys of Blue Hill* and *The Battering Ram*, which was his father's favourite tune. "He looked at my father, and said there is no way I am going to let him go. Let me take him back to England with me for six months and I'll make the best piper ever out of him."

John's pride in the Doran tradition is reflected in the following story During a visit to County Clare in 1970 in the company of his uncle, Paddy Doran; they arrived in Miltown Malbay, pulled up in the street and asked a man where the piper Willie Clancy lived. The man said "What's your name, "My name is Doran," said Paddy. "Patrick Doran. Paddy Doran." "The Dorans are back, the Dorans are back!", cried the excited local.

We then went on to visit Willie Clancy's widow, and she told us that almost every morning Willie would tell her that he dreamt of Johnny Doran during the night. Rooney claimed that he never forgot a good tune, and he also never forgot a good story, confirming what Mrs. Clancy had told him. (Rooney, J. Manchester, 2010)

Rooney recalls Martin Rochford, the Co Clare fiddle and uilleann pipe player who was a great friend of the Dorans, explaining how important it was for local musicians to persuade the famous piping brothers to stay as long as possible, and the lengths to which they would go to ensure that they did. Johnny Doran had been camping

Figure 2 Paddy Keenan, John Rooney, Mickey Dunne, Johnny Purcell, Doran Tionól, Wicklow, Feb. 19th, 2000 (Picture courtesy of Na Píobairí Uilleann)

just across the road from Rochford's house. Doran was due to leave the following day, but that night Seán Reid, another great musical friend and admirer of the Dorans, and Rochford took Johnny's horses away across the fields, and hid them so well that Doran wasn't able to leave for another two weeks until he had recovered them. (Rooney, J. Manchester, 2010)

John Rooney's music

John is regarded by members of the Doran Traveller extended family as one of the leading exponents of the Traveller style of uilleann pipe playing. Based in north west England, he works at kerb laying as his primary source of income. His son Larry works with him and Larry, born in 1980, has developed into an excellent piper, playing in a true Traveller style, very much influenced by his father. John Rooney is a frequent visitor to Ireland, attending at least 7 of the 10 annual Doran Tionóls since its inception in 2000.

His playing is fast and full of attack, but never out of control. He deploys every device available to the experienced piper-rolls, cuts, crans, popping, piping and sliding, all on the chanter. His accompaniment on the regulators is relentless, and very much in the style of Johnny and Felix Doran. Rooney's chanter work is generally in the open style favoured by Felix, but used to good effect by Johnny, who moved easily between open and tight playing within any tune he has recorded. Rooney's regulator playing very closely resembles Felix's approach, constant vamping, emphasizing the rhythm, and not designed to add the melodic colour which was a characteristic of Johnny Doran's playing. He achieves the great volume required by his outdoor playing predecessors, pushing the pressure on the bag to the outer limits, just short of over blowing, and constant off-the knee playing which facilitates the open-end chanter to produce more volume.

Rooney is content and confident with a limited repertoire, almost exclusively drawn on the Doran catalogue, and including Traveller favourite reels such *Rakish Paddy, The Bunch of Keys, The Primrose Lass, The Bucks of Oranmore* and *jigs* including *Out in the Ocean, Rose in the Heather, Coppers and Brass* and *The Lark in the Morning*. John is oblivious to the current convention amongst traditional musicians of avoiding repeating a tune in a session, and merrily resorts to one of his favourites as often as the fancy takes him. The authors once counted him return to *Rakish Paddy* nineteen times during one session at the first Doran Tionól in 2000 in Wicklow.

One of traits so evident on that weekend was his generosity to children of non Traveller parents, aspiring young pipers keen to imitate the Traveller style. Over the weekend Rooney's patience with the young pipers was evident to all, as he invited them play with him. His generosity and temperament when instructing his young audience on how to master the quick regulator work which was such a feature of the Dorans' playing, was a joy to behold.

He was a gentle giant whose presence filled the room, and his quick wit and general good humour during that special, inaugural weekend made it a memorable experience for everyone who came in contact with him. In later years when Rooney arrived at the Doran Tionóls with his young son Larry, it was very evident that a very special bond was in existence between the two of them. And as they played pipes together, father and son driving out tunes, with Johnny also shouting encouragement at Larry during the tune, it was magical to hear and riveting to observe.

Recognised throughout Ireland and England by those associated with Irish music, John Rooney is an institution carrying with him a proud tradition handed down from generations of Dorans and Cashes, and passing on the legacy to his sons and to any young piper who is willing to learn from him. The Doran generosity is so much a part of his life and he regards music as an inheritance that must be passed to the younger generation.

The Doran weekends are now held every year in Spanish Point in Co Clare and it is a very cherished annual event for those who attend to hear the Dorans, Rooneys and Purcell. But all agree than on the few occasions when John Rooney is absent, there is a void and his presence is sorely missed.

John Rooney, and his wife Bridget, Manchester, 2009
(Courtesy of Tommy Fegan)

Chapter 11: Johnny Purcell

Johnny Purcell, with Noel Fitzgerald, Doran Tionól, Spanish Point, Co Clare, April, 2010. (Courtesy of Tommy Fegan)

Johnny Purcell, grandson of Johnny Doran, is the only direct descendant of the legendary uilleann piper who plays pipes. He was born on 31 May, 1960 in Liverpool to Paddy Purcell and Nan Doran, daughter of Johnny Doran. The family returned to Ireland shortly after he was born, and they travelled throughout Ulster and Leinster, as Paddy supported his family by providing tarmacking services. In 1976, at the age of 16, Johnny left Ireland and emigrated to England to build his own business as a Traveller tradesman.

Johnny first heard about the uilleann pipes when he was a child, listening to his father, Paddy Purcell, at sessions in pubs, talking about Felix and Johnny Doran. His uncle, Handley Doran, who was a son of Johnny Doran, played a little on the pipes and Handley encouraged his young nephew to play. Handley had a copy of the tape of *The Bunch of Keys*, the only recording of his grandfather, Johnny Doran, playing

the pipes, and Purcell first heard it in the early 1980s. He was totally in awe of his grandfather's style of playing, deciding instantly that he wanted to learn to play the pipes. From then on, Johnny has been dedicated to playing pipes in the Travellers' style.

Mikey Doran Sr, son of Felix Doran, and John Rooney were the first two pipers Purcell ever heard playing live, about 1987. He taught himself to play, mainly from listening to the recording of his grandfather, and from listening to Mikey Doran and John Rooney. He got his first practice set of pipes from the late Dave Williams, the maker of choice for most Traveller pipers. He listened closely to the playing of his grandfather Johnny Doran, and tried to assimilate the sound into his own playing. He received no formal lessons or even tips passed on and Johnny was left very much to his own devices. Johnny taught himself the basics of reading music, and with a combination of listening to others and the tape of his grandfather, he developed his own style and repertoire.

He attended the Piper's Club in Leeds a few times, but due to his nomadic lifestyle, he was unable to attend there on a regular basis. He acquired his first full set of pipes in the early 1990s, but again, due to the demands of travelling, he didn't play them in earnest for at least another four years.

The occasion of the annual Doran weekends, beginning in 2000 in Wicklow, motivated him to take the pipes more seriously, and he began to practice in anticipation of the annual event. Purcell gradually modelled himself on Felix's style of playing, and deliberately cultivated the Traveller approach to playing music. The annual Doran weekends were very important to his commitment to the pipes, and he was conscious of the expectation that non-Travellers had of his commitment to his grandfather's legacy.

Johnny Purcell acknowledges that the continuation of the Doran legacy rests firmly with Mikey Doran Jr, and Larry Rooney, and he hopes that their children in turn will also make that commitment. Johnny owes a great debt of gratitude to John Rooney, for maintaining the Traveller style of piping over many years. Purcell regards John Rooney as the lead custodian of that tradition, and he appreciates the impact the Doran weekend had on his motivation and commitment to playing the pipes;
"The Doran name would be gone if it hadn't been for the Doran weekend. John (Rooney) keeps playing and he keeps the sessions going. He has done a lot over the years, in all fairness to him." (Purcell, J. Manchester, 2010)

Johnny likens the impact the Dorans made on piping to the influence of Rolls-Royce had on car making. "The Dorans were like the old guys, Mr Rolls and Mr Bentley." He recognises that life has changed for Travellers, but he is hopeful that the Travellers' style of piping will live on. He acknowledges the efforts of pipers such as Paddy Keenan,

Johnny's son, Henry Purcell-Great-grandson of Johnny Doran
(Courtesy of Johnny Purcell)

Finbar Furey, John Rooney, young Mikey Doran, Larry Rooney, and non-Travellers who are leading exponents of that style, such as Michael O'Connell and Pat Broderick. He is also very conscious of his own direct lineage from Johnny Doran, and his hope is that he may be able to keep that legacy alive;

"My son, Henry, is 14. I have tried a few times, and he probably may get around (to playing). But he doesn't and you can't force them to play. I'll maybe give my pipes to some young fella who wants to play, I don't know, I can't force him so I think for the music they have to have their heart in it. You've got to like it, like the opera. I hope that someday someone belonging to me will play. I've got some stuff from a fellow, Leo Purcell, who used to live in Dublin. He has moved to Michigan, inland America, and you can get him on the Internet. He is a teacher of music. He sends people to Ireland who won all Ireland championships. He could be related to Johnny." (Purcell, J. Manchester, 2010)

Johnny is delighted that the research for a book is being done, as he believes that there are lots of people, including Travellers, who wouldn't know about the Dorans. "It's a good thing; it is there for life, and everyone including my mother is very proud of that."

Johnny Purcell's Music

Although Johnny is a grandson of Johnny Doran, his music more closely resembles the playing of Felix Doran. He has Felix's steadier rhythm, less racy than Johnny's and less ornamented. Almost all of his chanter playing is in the open, legato style, which facilitates the free flowing approach to his music. Purcell is in control of the tune as he allows the chanter work to create a sense of ease and fun, devoid of the challenges of tighter music. His regulator playing is firmly rooted in the Traveller style, bouncing and in constant use, creating a very pleasing sense of enjoyment for the listener.

His repertoire is consistent with the tunes played by the prominent pipers of the Travellers' tradition, including the *Ash Plant, Rakish Paddy, Primrose Lass, Swallow's Tail* and *The Congress* reels. The jigs in the Traveller repertoire which Johnny Purcell regularly performs includes *Out in the Ocean, The Lark in the Morning, Coppers and Brass,* and *Tripping it up the Stairs.*

His approach to playing is less visually exciting than that of his peers, such as John Rooney and Paddy Keenan, but his contribution to any session is constant, dependable and sustaining. He enjoys picking up tunes outside the normal repertoire of Travellers, and every Sunday he exchanges tunes with Tommy Fegan over the mobile phone. He often plays his low D whistle during these telecommunications sessions, as it is more readily available when the impulse to play a tune during a call arises. His travelling circuit (throughout England, Scotland and occasionally to Holland) is geographically more widespread than Rooney's, and he avails of the opportunity to call into sessions wherever his work takes him. Such opportunities extend his repertoire beyond the stable diet of Traveller tunes. Johnny Purcell is generous with his music and will take time after a session to pass on a tune to anyone who asks. He is proud of his heritage and never fails to play or discuss the Irish Traveller uilleann pipe tradition of his grandfather and great-granduncle, Johnny and Felix Doran.

Neilidh Mulligan and his brother Alphie examine Felix Doran's Silver Set, and the set Felix sold their father in the 1960s. Tadhg Mulligan and Mickey Sr look on. Doran Tionól, Spanish Point, 2010. (Courtesy of Leo Rickard)

Chapter 12: Simon Doyle

"This my music" (Simon Doyle, Manchester, 2010)

Simon Doyle and family, Manchester, October 2010. (Courtesy of Tommy Fegan)

Simon Doyle was born in Manchester on 3rd August, 1972. His father, Joe Doyle, was a Traveller, originally from the Country Longford area, and his mother was Winnie McDonagh from County Kildare. Simon first heardIrish traditional music when he was seven or eight years of age, listening to his father, "who did a little bit of lilting." He also played "a small bit on the tin whistle". His father bought him a tin whistle around this time, and he started off by learning a few notes. He went to sessions in Manchester, and initially listened to his eldest sister, Winnie playing the fiddle. He also listened to a number of pipers and records which his father had. He went on to learn the flute when he was about 15 or 16 years of age, and started playing the uilleann pipes when he was 18. His father was friendly with Felix Doran and he often told young Simon stories about Felix. Doyle first heard tape recordings of Felix when he was in his early 20s, but he also heard his father lilting Felix's tunes. Many of the tunes that he plays were learned directly from his father's lilting of Felix's tunes. When he got his first set of pipes, he tried to learn from music books,

but he could not understand the written notation. His father said, "Books are no good, there are plenty of tips there, but you need to get on to the music and listen to it : Paddy Keenan, Tommy Keane, Finbar Furey." (Doyle, S. Manchester, 2010)

In later years he listened to tapes of Johnny and Felix Doran. He got married when he was 20 years of age. With a young family on the way, Simon applied himself to earning a living from buying and selling furniture to support them, and wasn't able to concentrate on the pipes until a few years later.

He moved to Ireland in 2004, and three years later he resumed playing the pipes, trying to tune them up. At this stage, he still had not received any formal lessons on the pipes, but was keen to meet the famed Traveller piper, John Rooney;

"We pulled into a camp, in Rumford, with a few of my cousins. I had

Mikey & Joe Doyle, Manchester, 2010, playing two practice sets made by Mickey Dunne.
(Courtesy of Simon Doyle)

a few drinks, and one of my cousins turned around and said, 'Felix Doran's son, Joe, is down in the other field.' I was only after getting the tapes of Felix and Johnny, and I was delighted. I was talking to Joe and he asked me if I played the pipes and I said that I did, and that I had his Daddy's tapes. I gave him a copy, and he went back down to his trailer that night. He came back up to my own trailer in the next morning, with three car loads of family to hear me play." (Doyle, S. Interview, Manchester, 2010)

Joe told Simon that John Rooney had just pulled out of the camp three or four days prior to Simon arriving. Simon had three small children at the time, and was unable to catch up with Rooney until 2007 at the Doran Tionól in Spanish Point in County Clare. "We were criss-crossing; and every camp I was pulling into, he was pulling out." "There was a wanted poster on the road for me, like Jesse James," interrupted John Rooney. (Rooney, J. Manchester, 2010)

Simon's young children are all playing Irish traditional music, or, as in the case of the two youngest, will be playing when they are old enough. Winnie Marie, 17, plays banjo, Bridget, 16, plays accordion, Margaret, 12, plays fiddle, and the two younger boys, Joe 10 and Mikey 9, have been playing practice sets of uilleann pipes, made by Mickey Dunne, Limerick, for over two years. His twins, Simon and Christopher, aged 7, will be starting on uilleann pipe practice sets soon. His two youngest daughters, Mary-Jane, 4, and Sarah, 2, will have to wait a few years until they are big enough to be able to hold an instrument. Simon and his children play music every second night together at home, and they regularly attend sessions in Preston, Manchester and Liverpool.

Simon Doyle's Music

The most significant influences on Simon Doyle's music are the recordings of Johnny and Felix Doran. Before he was introduced to these tapes, in his early 20s, Simon had been trying to learn music from tapes and books, as well as learning directly from his father's lilting. For a while he tried to teach himself to read music notated in manuscript form, but soon discarded this approach in favour of depending on his aural instincts. On hearing the Dorans' music, he quickly abandoned any attempts at playing in a tight style, and

adopted a more open free flowing approach, a characteristic of Felix's music. The Traveller influences of Finbar Furey and Paddy Keenan can be heard in both his music, and his repertoire.

Simon is passionately committed to Irish traditional music, and he is keen to ensure that his young family becomes immersed in that tradition.

Chapter 13: Maggie Barry (1917-1989)

Felix Doran, Michael Gorman, Maggie Barry, Keele Folk Festival, 1965
(Courtesy of Brian Sheul)

Maggie Barry was born on 23rd January, 1917 in Peter Street, Cork and was christened Mary Margaret Cleary. Her parents were Charles Power and Mary Cleary, both of whom were musicians, but they were not Irish Travellers. According to Paddy Barry, her grandson, Maggie's paternal grandmother may have been a Romany Gypsy, and she was married to Robert Thompson originally from Lisburn, Co Antrim. Thompson was, by all accounts, an extraordinary uilleann piper who won the first Feis Ceoil in Dublin in 1897 and again in 1898 in Belfast, after which the rule barring winners from competing the following year was established.

She promoted her professional career as Queen of the Gypsies, even though she did not meet any of the criteria applicable to membership of the Irish Traveller community. Margaret Cleary was

therefore neither an Irish Traveller nor a Gypsy, even though she fully embraced for many years the lifestyle of an Irish Traveller and the image of a Romany Gypsy. Reg Hall, the folklorist, collector and record producer, who produced *Her Mantle so Green* (Topic Records, 1994), claimed; "Margaret's parents and uncles, with roots in street music, were musicians in the urban working-class tradition of the time, and, in the 1920s, her father played for the silent pictures and in a back street dance hall in Cork city."

Margaret Cleary left home around 1933, aged just 16, after a domestic dispute with her stepmother, and embarked on a career as a travelling minstrel, initially leaving on a bicycle, and eventually living in a traditional horse-drawn caravan. She travelled throughout Ireland, favouring the border counties on the eastern seaboard, and earned a reputation as a strong and versatile singer with a great panache for entertainment. Margaret accompanied herself on a five string banjo, performing popular folksongs of the time. She learned songs from various sources, and one of her most famous and enduring favourites, *My Lagan Love*, was learned by lingering outside a record shop long enough to listen to the song until she had it memorized. (Hall, R. 1958. *Her Mantle so Green*, Topic Records)

Robert 'Bob' Thompson, Maggie's paternal grandfather.

For almost 20 years, from 1933 to 1953, she travelled the length and breadth of Ireland, playing at fairs, markets and football matches performing popular folk ballads and earning a good living. She quickly gained a reputation as a very popular entertainer.

She married Charles Power, and they had one daughter, Nora, who was born in Mullingar in 1935. Nora later married Paddy Barry, and the young couple settled initially for a while in Creagganbane, Crossmaglen, in South Armagh, and eventually in Lawrencetown, Co Down. Maggie stayed with her daughter and son-in-law intermittently. For reasons unknown even to her family, Maggie Power, née Cleary, took the surname of her son-in-law, and became known to the world thereafter as Maggie Barry.

Seán Ó Boill, the Co Armagh school teacher and folklorist, met Maggie around 1951, and was influencial in arranging to have her recorded by Alan Lomax, the infulential ethnomusicologist and Peter Kennedy, the English folklorist and the popular *As I Roved Out* radio programme, for the BBC in Dundalk and London. A few years later she joined forces with Michael Gorman, (1895-1970) an outstanding fiddle player from south Sligo, the cradle of the cream of fiddle and flute players, many of whom went on to stamp an indelible mark on the future direction of Irish traditional music, via the economically enforced route of emigration to New York in the early part of the 20th century. Gorman, unlike many of his famous relatives and neighbours, such as Michael Coleman and Jim Morrison, choose the emigration path east instead of west, first to Scotland and eventually to London. In the aftermath of the Second World War, Gorman and countless other young men from the impoverished west of Ireland, sought a living and livelihood in the rebuilding of post-war England. They attended to the boredom and loneliness of their enforced exile by finding solace in seeking out other traditional musicians, initially in the pubs that catered for the burgeoning Irish immigrants in north London, around Camden and Kentish Towns.

These lonely exiles relieved the tedium of the long weekends by gathering in pubs, and, initially apprehensively, producing their instruments and creating what was to become the uniquely Irish phenomenon of pub sessions. In a handful of bars, clustered mainly in North London, musicians like Gorman, Willie Clancy, John Vesey,

Tony McMahon, Bobby Casey and Martin Byrnes sought each other out, initially perhaps out of homesickness, but eventually to re-engage in their passion for Irish traditional music. Many of them gathered on Sunday mornings, and then increasingly on evenings during the week, to set the template for Irish pub sessions that have since been emulated the world over.

Into this august and revered coterie of settled male musicians, entered the flamboyant and irreverent, self-styled Traveller and Queen of the Gypsies, Maggie Barry.

Together, Gorman and Barry were the musical hosts of at least four weekly sessions in the Bedford Arms, Camden Town from the mid-1950s, earning a steady and sufficient income. Initially landlords were reluctant to pay musicians, but Barry forced the pace by doing the rounds of the pub with a collection bag after their performances, eventually embarrassing publicans into paying musicians. For the next few years, they dominated the Irish traditional music scene in London, with many young recently arrived musicians flocking to listen to and play alongside the legendary Gorman. The Sligo fiddler's reputation and repertoire was the initial main attraction, but Barry's skillful ,and to west of Ireland exiles, new and exotic five-string banjo accompaniment, and her increasingly popular ballads, became an attraction that equalled and complimented Gorman's status and attraction. A young Dubliner named Luke Kelly (member of The Dubliners, folk group), recently arrived off the boat from his native city, was taking note. While the folk revival of the 1950s was getting underway in both Britain and Ireland, Barry was emerging into something of a cult icon, encouraged by her self-proclaimed Gypsy image.

Reg Hall played piano at some of those early sessions. His recognition by TG4, an award of the Gradam Cheoil Musicians Awards in 2009 was for the lifelong contribution to Irish traditional music, and his recordings of musicians of London sessions in the 1950s. He recognised the growing phenomenon that was Barry;
"Several times during the evening, Margaret Barry got to her feet for a couple of songs, testing the tuning on the banjo and swapping banter with those nearby to cover her shyness. She stood with head held back and eyes focused somewhere in space and gave her very best performance as she did every time. What presence. What timing.

The sudden shifts of tone through the range of her voice sent shivers down your spine, and in typical understatement somebody would mutter 'Ah, she's a fair auld singer, right enough.' As she broke into the tremolo banjo statement to round off the song, the hush in the bar-room was broken by whoops and cheers and a round of applause." (Hall, R. 2001. *Michael Gorman. The Sligo Champion.*) Topic Records, London)

In 1959, Barry and Gorman accepted a tempting offer, reputedly to be up to £120 per week, to tour the dance halls of Ireland, and they moved back to Co Mayo. This was quickly followed by lucrative tours of America and Australia in the early 1960s. Barry did little to dampen the image of a hard drinking Traveller, which she exploited to good effect whenever the glare of the microphone or the TV camera fell on her. The singer, songwriter and author Ron Kavanagh vividly recalled her impact on a boisterous, mainly male audience;

"There was a no-frills intensity to her performance that could instantly silence even the most boisterous heckler." He went on: "Although a gentle lady in private, in public she had the reputation of a woman you didn't mess with. A striking performer, she had a huge voice that needed little amplification even in the largest halls, and a strident no-frills banjo style." (Kavanagh, R. 2006. *Irish Ways*. Proper Records)

While Gorman, who was 23 years older than the energetic and fun-loving Barry, found touring in America demanding, the arrangements suited her eminently. Americans took to her Gypsy image, and her raucous and exuberant style of performance, and Gorman was content to play second fiddle, literally to Maggie, reversing the emphasis of their London performances, where Barry's banjo and occasional songs provided back-up to Gorman's legendary fiddle playing.

Michael Gorman passed away in 1970, but Barry continued touring. Tommy Fegan recalls an unforgettable night in 1974 when she performed in Café Lena's, Saratoga Springs, upstate New York, America's oldest continuously operating folk coffeehouse. The clientele in that small, intimate café house had been spoilt by folk luminaries such as Bob Dylan, Arlo Guthrie, Ani DiFranco and many others over the years. Tommy persuaded a few car loads of friends to make the journey from Albany to hear the legendary Barry, who he heard briefly busking at Newry market as a 5-year old in 1957. She left her American audience of folk sophisticates spellbound. They simply couldn't get enough of her that night. I'm sure they thought she was from another planet". (Fegan, T. Camlough)

She continued singing until shortly before her death in 1989, at home with her daughter Nora, in Lawernstown, Co Down. Nora had eleven children to her husband, Paddy Barry. One of the children, also named Paddy, married Donna Campbell and today they live in Banbridge with their three sons, Martin, Conor and Declan. Paddy plays guitar and sings, and his sons are deeply committed to Irish traditional and folk music. Martin plays banjo, guitar and bodhrán, Conor plays banjo, mandolin and bazooka while Declan plays whistle and bodhrán. Their home is a music house, cluttered with memorabilia to the legend of Maggie Barry, of whom they are immensely proud. Her legacy is alive and well in her adopted Co Down.

Maggie Barry's Music

Maggie Barry popularised many old songs, such as *The Galway Shawl* and the *Turfman from Ardee*. Her repertoire contained a generous amount of northern songs, including *My Lagan Love* and *The Flower of Sweet Strabane*, in sympathy, perhaps with her grandfather's birthplace, and the area she adopted. Thanks to folklorist and collectors like Seán Ó Boill, Ewan McColl, Alan Lomax, Reg Hall and others, her songs and early recordings in the 1950s became a source of inspiration for younger ballad singers-in-waiting, such as Luke Kelly, who brought the 5-string banjo accompaniment to new heights of popularity with the Dubliners a few years later. (Kelly's posture, head flung back while at the height of the intensity of the song, was not unlike Barry's)

Michael Gorman composed the popular reel, *The Mountain Road*, the two-part version of which is ubiquitous in the repertoire of traditional musicians worldwide today. And over a period of years he added a third and eventually fourth, fifth and a sixth part. Maggie Barry, influenced and aided by his composition skills, composed the five part jig, the *Strayway Child* (entitled, reputedly, in her own image).

Her ability to accompany Irish traditional dance music on the 5-string banjo was, and is to this day, innovative and unique. It was an unlikely accompaniment to the ears of recently arrived exiles from the west of Ireland, steeped in the tradition of solo house performances. The heady noise and smoke-filled bars of post-war London demanded accompaniment to lift the delicate fingering of the fiddle player above the din, and Barry's attacking rhythms-resounding, tuneful and uplifting -were just the ticket!

In the more rarefied situation of the recording studio, her grasp of the demands of instrumental dance music withstood the test for the new form of accompaniment. Legendary players like Gorman, Felix Doran, Willie Clancy, Séamus Ennis, Tommy Maguire and Martin Byrnes-men who didn't suffer musical fools gladly-were proud to have recorded dance music to her accompaniment.

Paddy Barry, with sons Martin, Conor and Declan, Banbridge, Co Down, 2010.
(Courtesy of Paddy Barry)

The Straway Child

The Straway Child,
Composed by
Maggie Barry

Chapter 14: Mikey Doran Jr.

"I am very proud and lucky to be part of it. To be the descendent of some of the greatest pipers"
Mikey Doran Jr, 2010

Mikey Doran Jr & son, Mikey, Manchester, 2010.

It was his confidence and his maturity at the tender age of 13 years that first alerted the audience to the extraordinary attributes of young Mikey Doran Jr. He arrived at the Doran Tionól in 2002 in Glendalough, Co Wicklow with his father Mikey Sr, son of the legendary Felix Doran. Uilleann pipes in his hand, within minutes he was centre stage with some of the best pipers in Ireland and the tunes were flowing from him like cascades of water from a spring brook.

There were many things that struck us about this teenager; his good looks, his charm, his confidence, his maturity and above all his extraordinary ability as a piper. This 5th generation of an uilleann piping dynasty was a welcome visitor to the Doran Tionól in Wicklow, a piping festival held to honour his grandfather and granduncle,

Johnny and Felix Doran.

His presence, and that of his father Mikey Sr, added greatly to the weekend's festival and at every session during that weekend Mikey Jr drew gasps of admiration from his adoring audience. But it was his concert appearance on stage that night in the company of Kevin Rowsome, Pat Broderick, Michael O'Connell and Mickey Dunne that really sent out the signal that this young man was special.

Before he started to play, he told his audience he was proud to be invited to the Doran weekend. He spoke of the importance of his grandfather's music and he gave the reasons why it should be kept alive and nurtured for the next generation.

He proudly proclaimed, "I am the descendant of Felix Doran, the greatest piper in the world, and I am proud of that", thanking his dad for teaching him the pipes. He then proceeded to play, and suddenly there was an appreciation by the audience that they were indeed listening to a Doran, It was a hair-raising experience. His young years gave lie to his talent as the *Bunch of Keys, Cregg's Pipes* and *the Bucks of Oranmore* were delivered with gusto to an appreciative audience.

"I started at a young age. I was maybe 11 or 12, just messing about. My grandfather got a small set made for my father. John Rooney got them for his son, Larry. We were in the pub with John Rooney and my daddy, and they were playing music, and these little small set of pipes came out. It struck me that I couldn't have them, because they were Larry's. We had a bag and chanter back home that my father got for my brother Felix when he used to play, years ago. I got them, and my father started me off. I think the first tune was the *Green Groves of Éireann*. The second one was *The Bucks of Oranmore*. My father threw me into the deep end."

"No one in my family reads music. Everything is by ear. At that time, I didn't have an ear for music. He would play the tune on the whistle, and I would watch his fingers. He would show me six notes at a time, and after a few months I progressed. I was then beginning to get the ear." (Doran, M. Manchester, 2010.)

Mikey didn't appreciate how good his grandfather's tapes were until he started playing himself. "Johnny and Felix were the Rolls-Royce of piping." He played the practice set for two or three months, and, still aged 12, moved on to a Kennedy full set which his father had. He had a lot of problems with that set, and, even at that early age, he was not satisfied with the tuning or the tone he was getting from the pipes..

"My golden moment was when I went back to the Doran weekend in Glendalough, and Dave Williams, the pipe maker was there. As he viewed the sparkling array of Williams sets been played by the other pipers, he called Williams over and said "Dave, we need to talk." That first Doran weekend introduced him to music in a more serious way. He looks forward to the Doran weekend every year, and is fully appreciative of the effort of the organisers Oliver O'Connell,

Mickey Dunne and Leo Rickard who are doing so much to keep the Doran legacy alive.

"The Doran weekend is the governing body that keeps the traditions of Felix and Johnny going. It is the headquarters of Felix and Johnny Doran. It is the living legacy. If we don't have that, we are bolloxed! Johnny and Felix will never be forgotten, but it is the Doran weekend that keeps it going. It is very important to try and keep the Traveller style of piping going."

Mikey is absolutely committed to ensuring that his young son, also named Mikey, will be a piper. "If you ask him what his name is, he will tell you. I am Mikey Doran the piper."

Later on that evening, as the session was in full flight, Tommy Fegan did ask young Mikey, aged three, what his name was. Without hesitation he replied, just as his father had indicated, "I am Mikey Doran the piper."

John Rooney, Mikey Doran Sr and Mikey Doran Jr, Manchester, 2009

Mikey Jr explained that even at the age of three, his son could differentiate between the music of Paddy Keenan and other pipers. Often, when travelling in the car, young Mikey would object if his father tried to take a Paddy Keenan tape out and replace it with another piper's. Mikey intends starting him on the whistle when he is four years of age, and progressing him onto the small practice set, made by Felix Doran, when he is six. With such encouragement, it is unlikely that the Doran dynasty will come to an end for at least another generation.

When talking to Mikey Jr at the end of that concert in Glendalough in 2002, the authors were impressed with his humility, his eagerness to share his stories and his complete dedication to the Doran piping tradition.

Mikey has been conscious from an early age of the importance of the Doran musical legacy, and he readily accepts the mantle that has been passed to them. In a radio interview with the BBC in Leicester, when he was 12 years of age, he reflected on his role in the preservation of the family tradition, with an acute sense of responsibility and a tinge of humour, which belied his young age;

"Then me grandfather taught me father and me father taught me. That's how I got my music. Felix was very famous, very well-known. One of the greatest in the world. He made hundreds of tapes. Just try and get your hands on one of them. One of them was *The Last of the Travelling Pipers*. Obviously that's not true now because I've just taken the business over. (Doran, M. Jr. Manchester, 2010)

Chapter 15: Larry Rooney

"Keeping the flame burning".

Larry Rooney at Spanish Point, Co. Clare, 2009 (Courtesy of Leo Rickard)

At the Doran uilleann piping Tionól in Glendalough, Co Wicklow in February 2002, a young man, aged about 13 years was sitting in the bar of the hotel playing the *Lark in the Morning*, a famous jig associated with the Doran family. His fair hair was covering his eyes and the beads of perspiration were dropping from his cheeks as he gave full vent to this magnificent tune.

The crowds, who were gathering around, were awestruck with his piping ability, and it was only when they saw John Rooney sitting close to him and barking out instructions to use more regulators that it became obvious that this was Larry Rooney, John's young son and grandson of the great Felix Doran.

He was captivating to watch, and the tone and sound of his pipes were loud and crystal clear as he worked his way through a half dozen tunes, constantly looking to his dad, who was intently watching his every move. Larry was working his audience into frenzy with his playing, and though he appeared to be very shy and quiet, he certainly could play music in the famous Doran tradition.

He did not say much during breaks in the music. He just absorbed the atmosphere that he had created by flicking his head as he brushed the perspiration from his forehead.

There was something quite unique about seeing such a young boy in complete control of a full Dave Williams set of uilleann pipes, playing the instrument in a manner that contradicted his young years, and at various sessions during that memorable night, he held his own with some of the best pipers in Ireland.

There was an air of excitement when his father John picked up his own pipes and father and son began to play a selection of reels, the *Primrose Lasses*, *Cregg's Pipes*, and *The Bucks of Oranmore*, and both father and son delivered a performance with a ferocity and passion, as if their very lives depended on the volume and speed of the tunes.

In previous chapters in this publication, the authors have touched on the volume of the music that was so much a trait of the Traveller musician, which enabled them to be heard above the noise of crowds at fairs and matches when they busked. On that night in February in Wicklow, young Larry Rooney, and Doran's grandson brought that Traveller trait to life.

Larry was a regular attendee at the Doran Tionóls in subsequent years in Wicklow and in Clare, The authors have had the pleasure of observing this young teenager grow into a fine young man over the years. He got married at a very young age to one of the Dorans, he now lives in Wales and thankfully he is continuing the piping tradition of his ancestors, Felix and Johnny Doran, his uncle, Mikey Doran and his dad, John Rooney.

"My daddy learned me the pipes, and he told me that the Doran's were the best pipers. I'm proud of the tradition and I'm proud of the Doran's. My Daddy makes sure that I play as often as I can, and he learned me everything." (Larry Rooney 2004)

At the Doran Tionól concert in Feburary, 2003, Larry Rooney and his young cousin Mikey Doran , also aged 13 years, performed together and it was incredible to watch two children, both first cousins and grandsons of a famous piping dynasty, electrifying an audience with their incredible skill.

In April 2008, Larry was at the Doran weekend in Spanish Point, and the maturity in his playing was evident to all who first meet him in Wicklow five years earlier. His rhythm, regulator work and chanter control was on a par with pipers many years his senior. In the Bellbridge Hotel session with Michael O'Connell and Hugh Healy two fine young Co Clare musicians, Larry Rooney delivered a magical performance that impacted hugely on his appreciative audience.

The temperature in the bar on that night was raised substantially by the piping skills of young Larry Rooney. It was also fitting that he was producing his best piping on the very spot in Clare where his grandfather and his granduncle played some 70 years earlier.

When he performed in concert that night with Finbar Furey, Mickey Dunne, Paddy Keenan and his dad John Rooney, the audience was witness to an unusual event. These four families from a proud Traveller background had come together to keep alive the Traveller piping style, handed down from John Cash. Irish culture and Irish music owes a debt of gratitude to John Rooney for passing the flame to his son Larry.

Larry joined us in Manchester in December 2009 on the stomping ground of Felix Doran and again with his cousin, Mikey Doran Jr. He produced an electrifying performance that would have had his grandfather Felix smiling broadly from the heavens. It is fair to assume that Felix would be proud of the piping legacy carried on in the Doran tradition by Larry Rooney, the boy wonder from Wales.

Larry Rooney at Spanish Point, Co. Clare, 2009
(Courtesy of Leo Rickard)

Chapter 16: William 'Bigfoot' Dundon

William 'Bigfoot' Dundon, Doran Tionól, Spanish Point, Co Clare, 25 April, 2010. (Courtesy of Tommy Fegan)

William Dundon was born in a trailer in Hackney, London on 26 November, 1988. His mother is Nellie Hanrahan, and his father is Willie 'Smiler' Dundon, who was born in Dublin. Smiler's mother was Anne Doran, a daughter of Jim Doran, who was an uncle of the pipers Felix and Johnny Doran. William's mother gave birth to eleven children, but nine of them died at birth. His only surviving sibling is his brother Jimmy. In 1990, when William was two years of age, the family moved back to Tallaght, Dublin where they lived until he was eight years of age. They then moved across to the east side of Dublin where they stayed until he was twelve years old, and then to Newry in Northern Ireland where they have been, on and off ever since. "I am a half Traveller and half settled" said William. William worked with his father from an early age, as they turned their hands to almost anything to earn a living. He left school when he was sixteen, and went on the road full-time with his father. He enjoys working with his father outdoors every day and continues to do so.

He first became aware of Irish traditional music when he returned to London for a weekend when he was thirteen years old. They went back to visit his mother's second cousin, Jimmy Hanrahan, better known as 'Black Jimmy' because he played a black accordion. Jimmy tried teaching him the accordion, but William was too young. But the experience kindled in him an interest in music which is his abiding driving force today. His interest in, and commitment to traditional music deepened at the age of fifteen, when he was living in Derrybeg in Newry. His father bought him his first accordion, which was a piano keyed accordion. He set about teaching himself but considering it to be too difficult, turning to the button row accordion which he found easier to play. William taught himself the basics of the accordion,

Johnny Purcell and William 'Bigfoot' Dundon, and 'Smiler' Dundon in background, Doyle's Pub, Camlough, Newry, Co Down, 2009. (Courtesy of Tommy Fegan)

and taught himself his first tunes. He learned these from listening to Radio na Gaeltachta, recording tunes that he liked and replaying them repeatedly until he had them note-perfect.

William first became aware of the famous Doran brothers through his aunt Maggie whose father, Jim Doran, was an uncle to Johnny and Felix Doran. Maggie introduced the Dundon brothers to the *Bunch of Keys* cassette recording of Johnny Doran, telling them that, "You're not Dundons, you're two little Dorans." Jimmy did not develop an interest in music to the same extent as William did, but he does play a little on the banjo, spoons and bodhrán. He also played the fiddle for a short period when they lived in England. A Scottish man named Burrows taught Jimmy a little on the banjo and fiddle. He doesn't have a fiddle, but often will borrow one at a session to play a few tunes. Jimmy married in 2008, and moved to Baltinglass, Co Wicklow with his new bride. Except for occasional sessions when William visits, Jimmy has not been playing much music since.

William's first exposure to a Traveller piper was when he met John Rooney in Nottingham in 2002, when the Dundons stayed with the Rooneys from Christmas Day to New Year's Day. John taught William many of his tunes, which William learned on the accordion.

William explains the process by which he learnt some of the tunes associated with the Dorans from John Rooney; I got *Cregg's Pipes* off him, but I had to slow it down in my head, because he goes a million miles an hour. I also got the *Maids of Mount Cisco*, and *The Maid behind the Bar*. I got them by ear, because I can't read music. I have to hear it once or twice, then it clicks in. It's like a little tape recorder inside my head; I listen to it, then its there for later on. (Dundon, W. Railway Bar, Newry, December 2010)

William also recalled that Rooney played *The Boys of Blue Hill* on the accordion during that visit. According to William, Rooney played the accordion before he played the pipes.

Rooney explained the basic functions of the pipes to William, and thus began his interest in playing the pipes. A few years later, around 2007, William started playing at the weekly session in the Railway Bar Newry. Playing every week with two of the local pipers, Tommy Fegan and the late Dermot Mackin, further developed his fascination with the pipes. Tommy encouraged him to consider the pipes, and brought him to the Doran Tionól in Spanish Point, County Clare in April, 2010. His fate was sealed, and shortly after his visit, William got the chance to purchase his first set of pipes from Bernard O'Hanlon, who has been runningIrish traditional music sessions in his bar O'Hanlon's in Mullaghbawn, South Armagh since the early 1970s.

William is very aware of the Traveller style of playing music. He appreciates the way John Rooney approaches his playing, adding in distinctive little pieces which makes the difference. William intends modelling his playing on the music of Paddy Keenan and Michael 'Blackie' O'Connell, one of the few non-Travellers who can play in the Traveller style of piping.

"I am very proud of it (Traveller style). If I can get it in my head, and start playing the Travellers' style, because I know I am playing in a style that is a settled sort of a way, and I definitely enjoy it. When I get going on the pipes, it is going to be a bit difficult, but I will sort it out, bit by bit". (Dundon, W. Railway Bar, Newry, December 2010)

Chapter 17: Joe Gaynor (1921-2002)

"Take me out of here Cathleen, I don't want to die here," pleaded the blind old man, as he groped his way along the unfamiliar corridor of a residential home in Dublin, where a relative, unable to cope, had arranged for him to spend his last days. Cathleen, a sister who was 21 years younger than him, did not know he was in the home, but Joe asked the night watchman in the home to write a note to "Cathleen, Fatima", (not knowing that Fatima was in Dundalk), asking her to come and rescue him. The letter was delivered, Cathleen came, and she took him out over three weekends, and then took him out to stay permanently with her and her husband, the late John-Joe Gaffey, and their family in Fatima, Dundalk.

During the three short years left to him before he died, Joe recaptured some of his former spirit and zest for life, entertaining the neighbours on the street with his extensive repetoire of tunes on the accordian, which included a broad spectrum of Irish traditional music, Scottish, opera, classical and country and western music. There are no commercial recordings ever made of Joe, and those charged by the state to record Irish traditional music for the national archives from the 1940's on, did not notice Joe, or, for that matter, the Raineys in Connemara or even earlier, Johnny Doran. The riches these Traveller musicians left the nation, from their tents in Galway, are in sharp contrast to the debt, poverty and distress, for generations to come, left by privileged party goers other tents erected at the Galway races during the Celtic Tiger years.

Joe Gaynor and Paddy Keenan, Galway.

Joe Gaynor was born in Bray, Wicklow in 1921, and was blind from childhood, but he was well possessed of the inner strength needed to overcome such disability, and he worked hard to become a fulltime traditional musician. He busked initially as a child in the small rural villages of east Galway, and eventually taking up a permanent residence outside some of Galway's most fashionable shops, for over 50 years. He could play fiddle, mouth organ, keyboards as well as the accordion. He could even play the mouthorgan or a tin whistle through his nose and the accordion with his feet. His musical tastes weren't confined to his native music, as he was equally versatile in opera and classical music, ensuring that he could entertain a wide spectrum of musical tastes, an important factor for a street performer in the demanding business of retaining the attention of the passing crowd.

As a child, Joe attended St Joseph's School, in Cabra, Dublin, a special school for blind children. According to his sister, Cathleen Gaffey, he was encouraged in his interest in music at this school. After a few years, he returned home to Galway, and travelled around Galway and Tipperary and other parts of the west. Cathleen's step-father, Jim Reilly, took good care of him, bringing him to fairs and markets all over the west. While Joe's brothers and sisters worked their way around the houses, selling craft goods and utensils, the young, blind

Joe Gaynor (Print courtesy of Barrie Maguire)

123

musician was left in the center of the town or village to busk. Joe's income always surpassed that of his brothers and sisters.

With the help of family members, he managed to continue travelling for some years, and played all over Ireland, and even spent a few years in permanent residence on O'Connell Bridge, Dublin. During his time in the capital, he was a regular visitor to the famous house sessions in "Radio Oranmore", the home of John Keenan and his musical family in Ballyfermot, Dublin. The Fureys, Dunnes and other great musical families frequented these sessions (Finbar moved in permanently for a few years).

"Joe lived in Oranmore Road in Ballyfermot with Michael and Kathleen Dunne, and he would busk on O'Connell Street. He was a gentle soul who could play many instruments and he also taught the accordion. I remember him well, one of nature's most lovable creatures". (Furey, F. Dublin 2011)

He eventually settled in Galway, living with a sister and her family in Henry Street. From there each morning he made his way to do a full day's busking on O'Brien's Bridge, then to a place outside Corbett's hardware shop in William St. He eventually moved to Glynn's Toy Shop, The Treasure Chest, in William St from where he entertained generations of Galwegians for over 30 years. During his early years in Galway, he took a break from the city streets each summer, and enjoyed the good weather and the convivial atmosphere playing outside the Banba Hotel in Salthill.

Joe is fondly remembered in Galway as a good natured, humorous and obliging individual who would happily play any tune requested by his admiring public. Business owners were delighted to have Joe's music enhance the ambiance on the street, and they were good to him, regularly providing him with beverages and refreshments (sometimes, in the frosty weather, lining his tea with a little drop of the hard stuff). Galway Taxis ensured Joe was left home safely to his family in Henry St. at the end of each day.

Joe inspired generations of young people, many of whom, like Noel Hill, world famous concertina player from Lissycasey, Co Clare, vividly remembers the positive impact Joe had on him on his visits to Galway as a child.

Tommy Fegan presenting the Barrie Maguire painting of Joe Gaynor to his sister, Cathleen Gaffey at the TARA Centre in Dundalk.

Renowned Traveller musician's local links

Press coverage of presentation of Joe's portrait to Cathleen Gaynor.(Courtesy of Dundalk Argus, June, 2010)

A visiting American artist, Barrie Maguire, photographed Joe on a trip to Ireland in 1999, and he created a painting based on this photograph which became the first in a remarkable collection of paintings and images of Irish life. When Tommy Fegan contacted Barrie and told him that Joe spent the last and happiest years of his life with his sister, Cathleen Gaffey, in Dundalk, and that she was attending adult education classes at the Tara Education Centre, Co Louth VEC, he readily offered to send a special painting of Joe. Cathleen was reduced to tears when a surprise presentation of a limited edition of the print was made to her in 2010.

It now occupies pride of place in Cathleen's beautiful home in Dundalk. Cathleen treasures Joe's memory, and she proudly displays Joe's instruments anytime visitors call. She is also so proud of her late husband, John-Joe, who made a home for Joe in his final years.

Joe Gaynor is perhaps one of Ireland's most unsung musical heroes. He rose above the disability of being born blind and the prejudices of the state and community against Travellers at that time. Through sheer persistence, Joe became a great and versatile musician, and brought joy to the thousands lucky enough to have heard him play in Galway, Dublin and other parts of Ireland where he travelled. Cathleen has some private recordings of him at home, including a recording of him playing with Jimmy Shand, the great Scottish accordion player. It is a pity the state bodies charged with preserving Ireland's musical heritage in the mid 20th century didn't pause a while to capture this incredible man's music for future generations.

Chapter 18: Musicians Influenced by the Traveller Style

There are many organisations and individuals from the settled community who actively celebrate and promote Irish Travellers' culture in general, and music and song in particular. Here we highlight some who are very enthusiastic about the legacy of Traveller uilleann pipe playing, and we want to pay tribute to them and others for their tireless efforts;

Michael O'Connell

Michael O'Connell from Co Clare, nicknamed "Blackie" because of his long black hair, is probably one of the finest young pipers on the traditional music scene today. Michael learned his craft from the Limerick Traveller piper Mickey Dunne, and he has modelled his style of playing on the piping of Mickey, Paddy Keenan, Finbar Furey and the Dorans. "I just love that free flowing, energetic way of playing where you can give full vent to your personality and just let the music flow. Today there is so much emphasis on technique and innovation that sometimes the music gets lost. Students are now playing with a ferocity simply because they can, and while there is no question regarding their talent, sometimes rhythm and moods are sacrificed for speed and technical skills that do nothing for the tune. If you listen to Keenan and Furey the music is always dominant and is never sacrificed." (O'Connell, M. Ennis, Co Clare, 2011)

Michael first heard John Rooney playing in 2000 in Wicklow town, and he loves playing music with him. Michael has combined his style of playing with the North Clare rhythm so closely associated with the Doolin and the Kilfenora area, renowned for set dancing. He has incorporated into this mix the Traveller style of piping taught to him by Mickey Dunne and influenced by the Traveller pipers.

Michael is a familiar face at sessions all over Clare, throughout the country and abroad, as he regularly teaches in America and gigs quite often in Europe. In Clare Michael can be found playing in McDermott's in Doolin, the Doolin Hotel, and in the Old Ground Hotel, the Usual Place and Considine's in Parnell Street, Ennis. Michael now is teaching the next generation of young pipers in Clare, preserving the piping tradition in a county so loved by the Doran brothers. There is now a rich vein of uilleann piping in the county with great young players like Tara Howley, Barry Heagney, Máirtin O'Coigligh, Sinead O'Halloran, Fergal Breen, Sean Lyons and Alex Carr. Michael fully recognises the extraordinary talents and legacy left to this generation by Irish Travellers. Another young musician greatly influenced by the Traveller style is Tadhg Mulligan, son of Dundalk-based piper Alphie Mulligan.

Micheal 'Blackie' O Connell. (Courtesy of PJ O' Connell)

The Piper
The man was a Facebook friend,
This man called Blackie with a long black ponytail and piercing black eyes
He was cramped in the noisy pub corner, among the drinking glasses,

laughter and friendly banter, beside a fiddle and a bodhran, a flute and an accordion.
Those pipes he wrung the wind from, lay lovingly arranged on his lap,
The bellows were strapped to his elbow and he breathed his surge of life into them
With the rhythm of his body as his arm pumped the air.
In penal times such men devised this method to foil the crown's petty laws
Designed to exterminate music from this rebel land,
when it could mean death to blow.
He hung the chanter across his chest, below his shoulder that's for sure,
So as not to infringe imposed height restrictions.
He could have been in damp green woods, where no harm would befall his instrument,
Where he could charm the breezes to surrender their strange lament.
He closed his eyes and like a shaman he passed beyond,
from where he hauled up all our sunken sadness and our pain,
till our vision to the other place where he communed on our behalf
Across the weaving knot centuries across the boggy land,
across the famine and the still black lough
From where he hauled up all our sunken sadness, and our pain
Till we became ecstatic in our power again.

(Written for Michael O'Connell by Deirdre McGarry, USA, 2011)

Pat Broderick

In Loughrea in Co Galway, on the road out of the town, there is a bronze statue of the piper, Patsy Tuohy another fantastic musician from the 20th century who performed his craft in the music halls in America. He was a contemporary of Michael Coleman and the Flanagan Brothers who were also trail blazers in Irish music in America.
Carrying on a proud tradition of uilleann piping in this part of East Galway is Pat Broderick, a wonderful piper,who like Michael O'Connell has adopted the travelling style of piping. Pat will readily admit to being totally influenced by Finbar Furey;
"When I first heard Furey playing, that was it for me, I couldn't get over the sound he produced on the pipes"

He is a close friend of Paddy Keenan, and they play music together

Pat Borderick, Doran Tionól, Spanish Point, 2010. (Courtesy of Leo Rickard)

when Keenan's global schedule permits. Pat is the son of Peter Broderick and nephew of Vincent Broderick, both of whom have composed some great traditional tunes. Pat's brother Val is also another uilleann piper, keeping the Broderick name to the fore in Irish music in East Galway. Pat is a regular at the Doran Tionóls and is happiest in the company of Rooney, Keenan, Purcell and the Dorans. Pat also teams up with Michael O'Connell regularly. He has never missed any of the Doran Tionóls since they started in 2000, and his presence provides an energy on which inspires the visiting Doran musicians.

Martin Nolan

Martin was born in Chapelizod in Dublin, Ireland, and he took his first lessons from John Keenan Sr, in Ballyfermot, a short journey Martin made by foot or on bike for weekly lessons on the pipes. Martin got his formal lesson from John, then immediately retired out the back of the house, to play that night's tune and others, with John's musical sons, Paddy, Thomas and Brendan. Martin recalls them often playing the one tune for 20 minutes, and in doing so he developed the ability to think of variations to give musical relief to the repetition. John's kindness was reflected in the fact that he insisted in driving the young piper home in his van if he stayed late playing with the boys.

Martin's playing is strongly influenced by the Traveller style of piping, which employs both legato and staccato techniques, elements which are heard to great effect in his playing.

He has successfully adapted uilleann pipe playing to other forms of music. While he is highly respected in the Irish traditional music circles, he has also played alongside jazz greats such as Dave Liebman, the late Michael Brecker, Ronan Guilfoyle, Conor Guilfoyle, Tommy Halferty, Michael Buckley and the Boclé Brothers. Other collaborative work includes virtuoso Hungarian violinist Zoltan Lantos and Japanese performance artist Keiji Heino.

Martin Nolan, Spirit of 66 Club, Belgium, 2010.
(Courtesy of Lutz Diehl)

In 2009, Martin joined the Celtic progressive rock band Iona, in which his pipes are a central feature. Martin's uilleann piping has taken him throughout Europe and the UK, India, Australia, New Zealand, the USA and Canada, from the Lincoln Centre for the Arts in New York to the national theatres of Ireland and England and concert halls across the Indian subcontinent. But his appearance at the Doran Tionól in Spanish Point in 2011 as Guest Artist confirms the respect in which he is held by his piping peers, and for the Travellers' piping tradition of which he is a great and proud exponent.

Joe Doyle

Joe Doyle is a Dublin based piper and is the featured teacher at all the Doran Tionóls. Some of Ireland's best pipers today at some point or another received coaching from Joe Doyle, and he is regarded as a patient, competent teacher with a huge love for all types of uilleann piping. He is an avid admirer of Patsy Touhy and the Traveller style of piping.

Joe Doyle (Courtesy of Leo Rickard)

Joe is a charismatic character with a wicked sense of humour, loved and respected by all musicians lucky enough to come into contact with him. He has enriched every piping Tionól and is a an inspirational teacher with kind words of encouragement for all aspiring young pipers. A piping weekend without Joe Doyle would just not be the same.

Leo Rickard

Leo Rickard, a native of Howth in Co Dublin, is one of Ireland's finest exponents on the uilleann pipes. Leo has a number of quality CD's to his credit, and along with his close friend Joe Doyle, has been a major influence on a number of young pipers. Leo is a member of Na Píobairí Uilleann and is also one of the main organisers of the Doran weekends in Co Clare. He is an avid lover of the Traveller style of piping, and is constantly promoting this unique piping craft. Leo is totally committed to preserving this piping tradition handed down from the Cashes and the Doran piping dynasty. Leo will admit to being heavily influenced by the piping of Paddy Keenan whom he has known since 1978. "Paddy's influence has been enormous and it is there today for all to see, he was a trailblazer" says Leo.

"It is so important that we keep this Traveller style of piping alive" says Leo," It is a cherished legacy and we owe it to the next generation to keep it alive".

Leo Rickard (Courtesy of Jim Fitzpatrick)

Brendan Collins and Joe Barry

Two wonderful Co Tipperary pipers Joe Barry and Brendan Collins, are regular visitors to the Doran Tionóls and were guest performers in 2011 at the Doran Weekend in Miltown Malbay. Both of them have a huge respect for the Traveller style of piping and are to the fore in the promotion of uilleann piping with the annual Tionól held every year in Templemore. They are keeping the flame alight in the Tipperary, a stomping ground of Johnny Doran who travelled all over the county in his annual trips to Clare and Galway.

Brendan Collins and Joe Barry

Sean McCarthy.

Sean is a young piper from North Cregg, Fermoy in Co Cork. He has been a regular attendee at all the Doran Tionols and was the featured guest at the Doran Concert in Co Clare. He is an exceptional piper and like many of his fellow pipers, he has been influenced by Paddy Keenan, the Dorans, and Eoin O'Riabhaigh the Cork Piper.

Sean has won a number of All Ireland titles on the pipes and has toured extensively bringing his music to International audiences. He has a huge appreciation of the style of piping handed down from generations of Traveller musicians to the settled community and he rates the Doran Piping Tionol as a must attend event every year.

Mark Redmond.

Mark is from Gorey Co Wexford and he developed his piping skills at the Doran Tionóls where as a young child he sat and played with the piping greats, John Rooney, Mickey Dunne and Paddy Keenan. Mark is now a fantastic piper and is hugely appreciative of the grounding he received from those Pipers at the Doran weekends. He was the featured guest at one of those piping Tionóls in Co Clare where he delivered a polished performance to an appreciative audience and he is hugely indebted for the wonderful piping legacy handed down from the Dorans, Cashes and the current group of travelling greats, Mickey Dunne, Paddy Keenan and Johnny Rooney.

.

Epilogue

This publication is a record of the contributions made by the travelling troubadours of Ireland over the last two centuries, and we acknowledge with gratitude the cultural legacy they left for future generations of Irish people.

Chapter 19: Transcriptions Of Tunes

This chapter includes a selection of transcribed tunes performed by Johnny Doran, Felix Doran, Ted Furey, Finbar Furey and Paddy Keenan.

The transcriptions provide the opportunity for readers to appreciate how Irish Traveller musicians interpreted traditional tunes. The tunes selected form part of a repertoire very closely associated with Irish Travellers, although these tunes are played by Irish traditional musicians worldwide. We appreciate that transcriptions cannot fully convey the spirit and soul of the music of the performer, and we encourage those wishing to understand the Irish Travellers' style of music to seek out recordings and, where possible, live performances.

We are particularly delighted to provide tunes transcribed by Ted Furey. These are a small section of tunes he collected over many decades, lovingly and colourfully transcribed by hand. Ted ensured the consistency of the size of the notes, by drilling a hole in a piece of Perspex, and using that for every note he transcribed in his collection. Comments on many of the tunes indicate the source and the year, providing an insight to his extensive travelling throughout Ireland, and the company of legendary musicians with whom he was associated. The complete manuscript has been donated by the Furey family to the Irish Folklore Commission, UCD, Dublin.

Time and space has precluded us from providing a more comprehensive collection of transcriptions of tunes played by Irish Travellers. We have already undertaken the transcription of the complete repertoire of Johnny and Felix Doran, which we will publish shortly.

Rakish Paddy

Johnny Doran

Rakish Paddy (An Píobaire, vol 2, no. 12, February 1982)

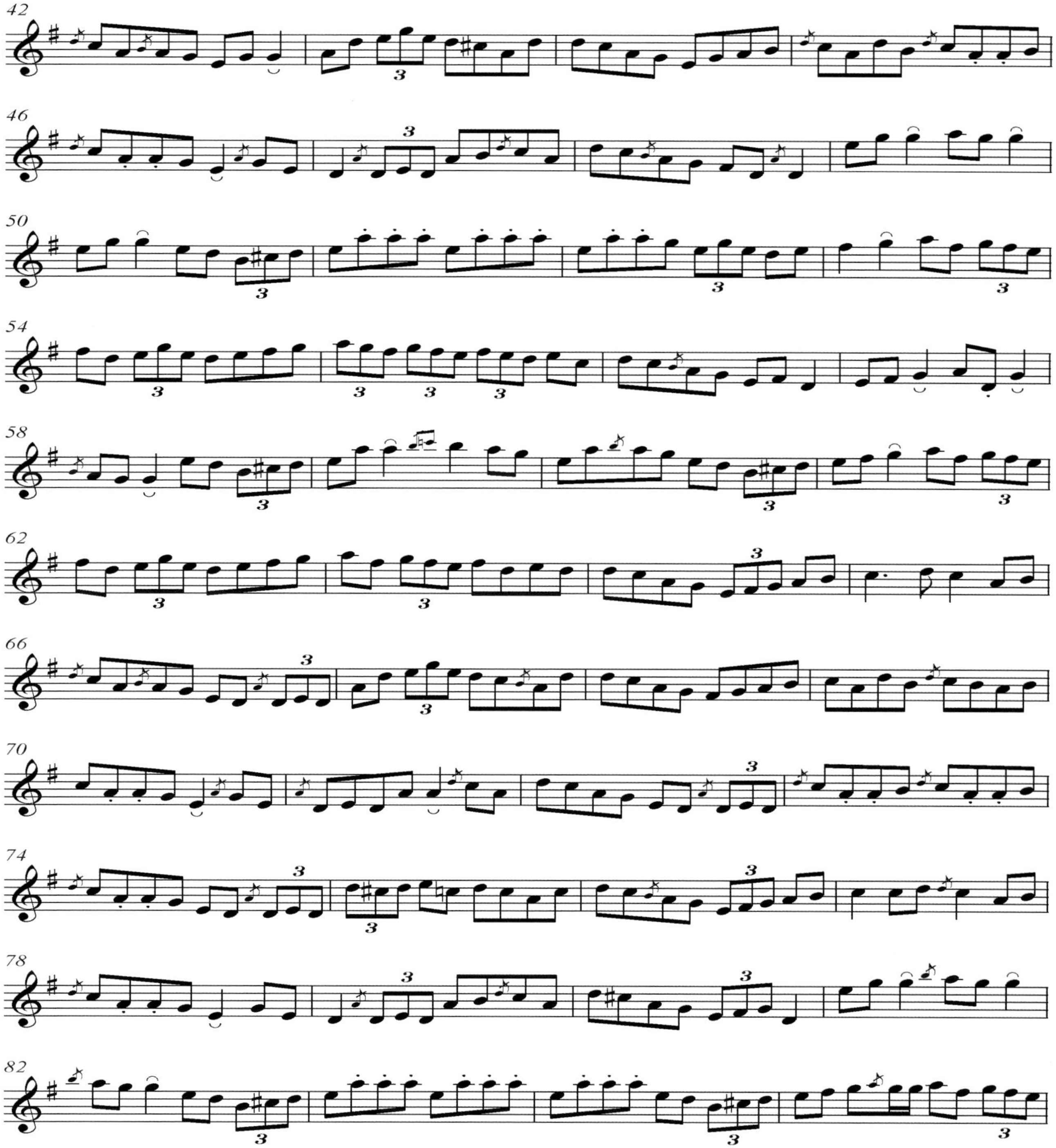
42
46
50
54
58
62
66
70
74
78
82

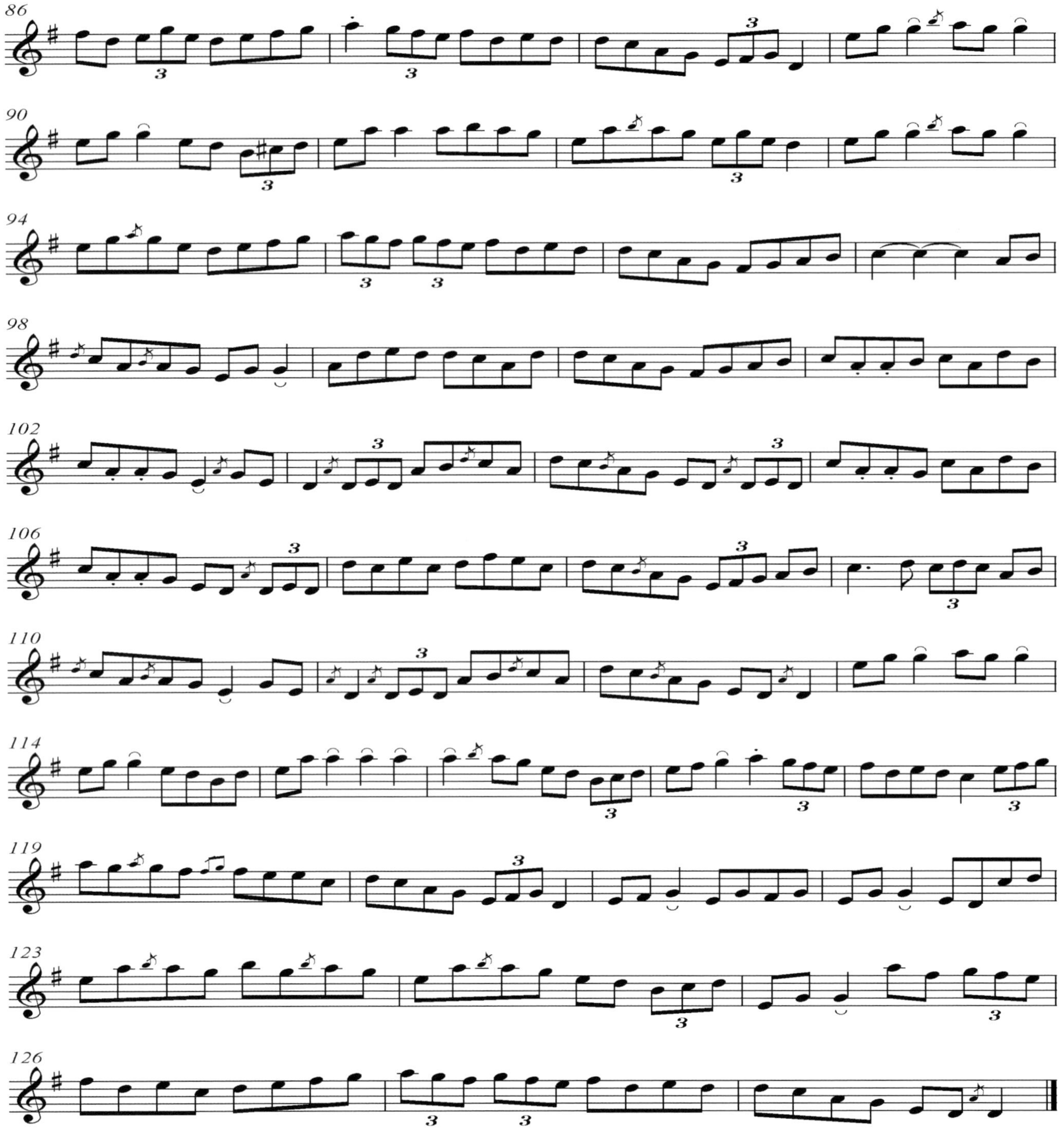

Colonel Frazer

Johnny Doran

Colonel Frazer (An Píobaire, vol 2, no. 30, May 1986)

Coppers and Brass

Johnny Doran

Coppers and Brass (An Píobaire, vol 2, no. 40, July 1988)

My Love is in America

Johnny Doran

My Love is in America (An Píobaire, vol 2, no. 31, July 1986)

The Bunch of Keys

Johnny Doran

The Bunch of Keys, 1st version, part 1 (An Píobaire, vol 3, no. 21, January 1995)

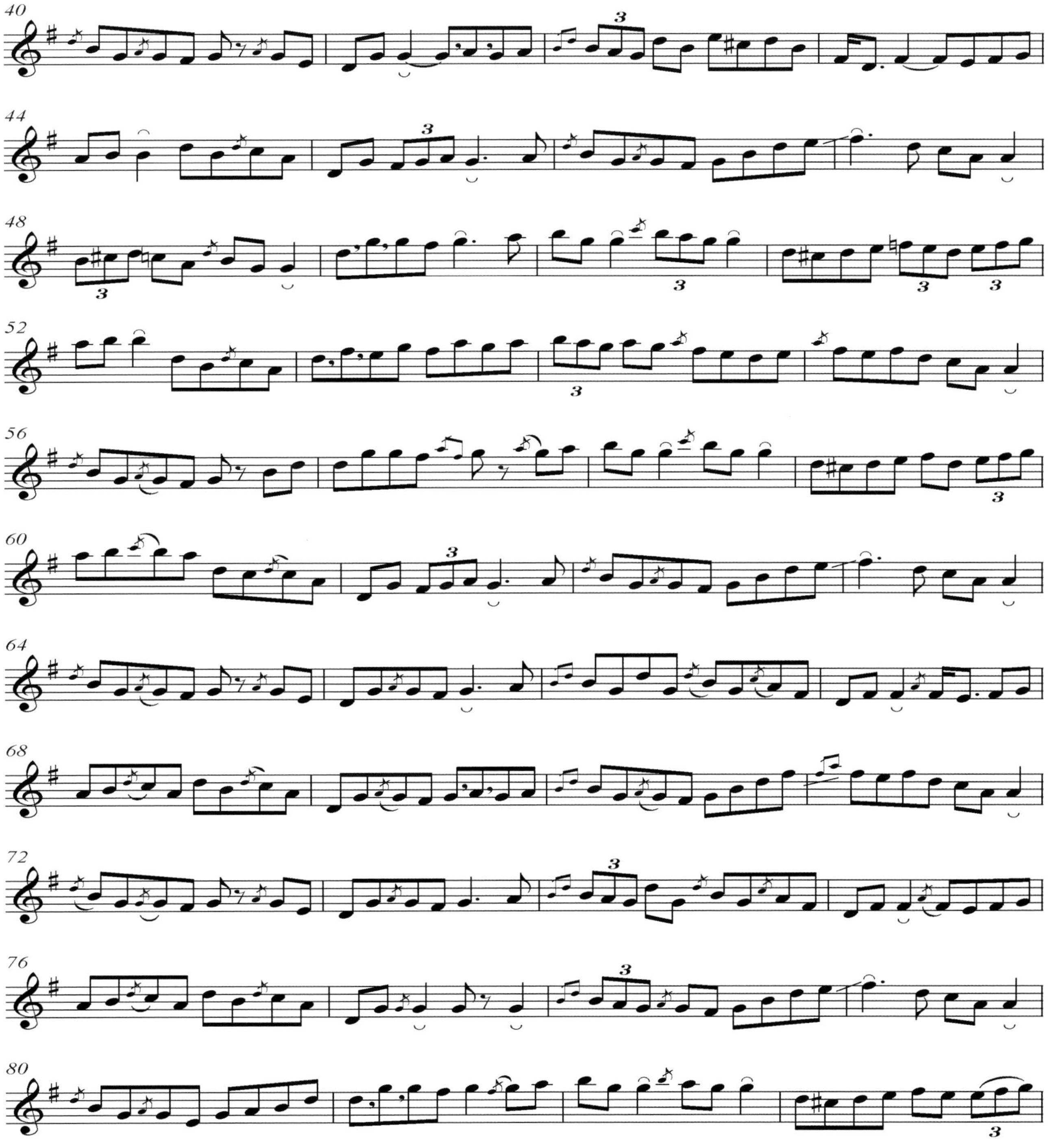

The Bunch of Keys
(Second Playing)

Johnny Doran

The Bunch of Keys, 2nd version (An Píobaire, vol 3, no. 22, April 1995)

The Blackbird

Johnny Doran

The Blackbird - part 1 (An Píobaire, vol 1, no. 29, March 1977)

The Job of Journeywork

Johnny Doran

Crumlish/Fegan

8

Primrose Lasses

Felix Doran

Transcribed by Jesse Smith

Rakish Paddy

Felix Doran

Transcribed by Jesse Smith

The Bucks of Oranmore

Felix Doran

Transcribed by Jesse Smith

2

The Fermoy Lasses

Felix Doran

Transcribed by Jesse Smith

McLeods

Paddy Keenan

Transcribed by Fegan/Mc Aufield

Steam Packet

Paddy Keenan

Transcribed by Fegan/MacAulfield

Hag with the Money

Transcribed by Fegan/MacAufield

Finbar Furey

Colonel Frazer

Finbar Furey

Transcribed Fegan/ McAufield

2

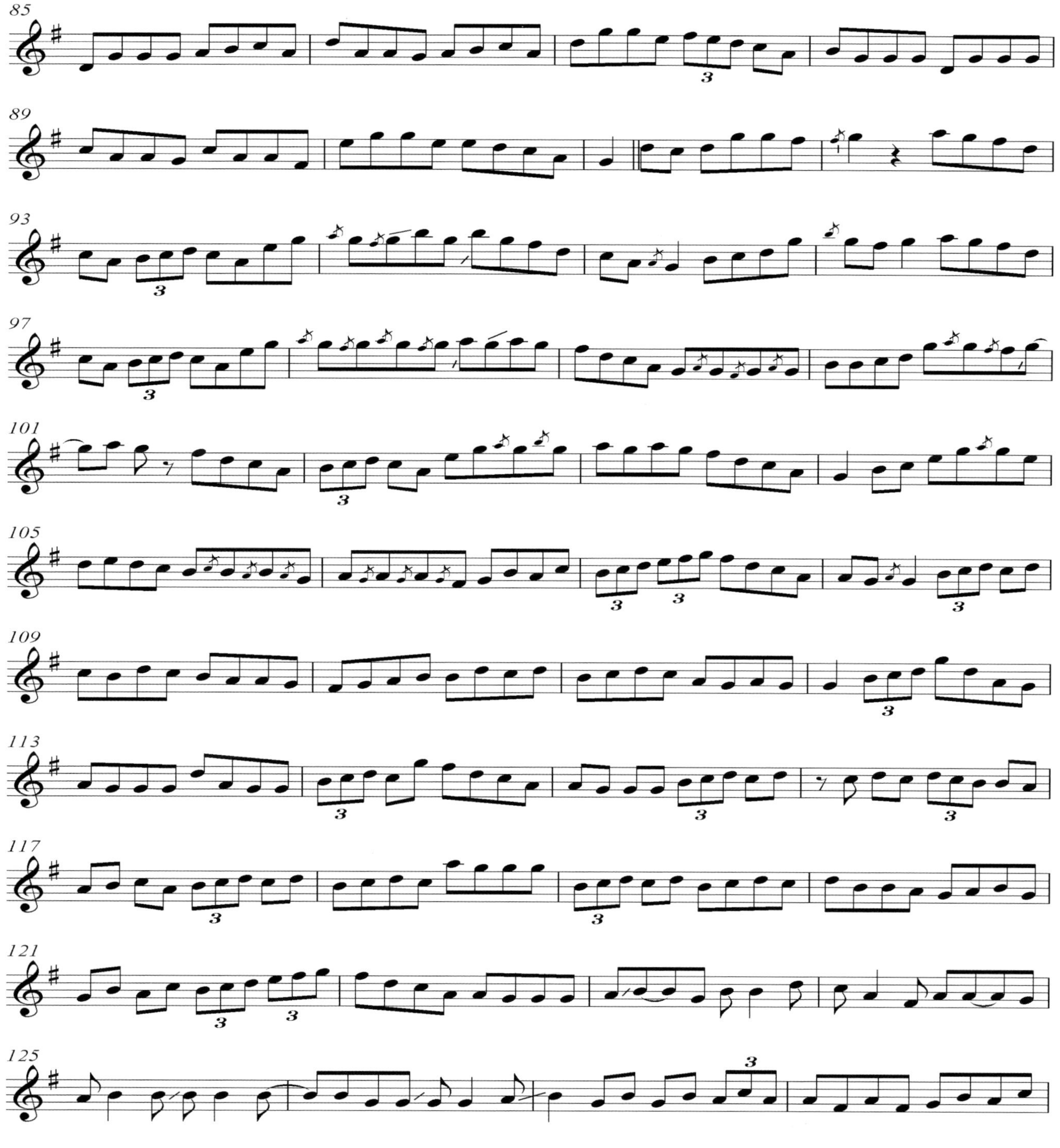

4

No.	Tune	No.	Tune	No.	Tune	No.	Tune
1	LORD GORDON	22	QUEEN OF THE — MAY —	43	KEER.UM — GOOR.UM	108	THE KERRY HORNPIPE
2	JENNYS Chickens	23	COLLEGE GROVES	44	WEST WIND	109	KITTY'S WEDDING
3	FLOGGIN REEL	24	ROSS BAY - REEL	45	MERRY BLACKSMITH	110	JOLLY TARS
4	BOYS O' THE LOUGH	25	O'DOWDS FAVORITE	46	BROKEN PLEDGE	111	REEVYS FAVORITE
5	TEASE THE FEATHERS	26	JENNYS WEDDING	47	MAUD MILLER	112	COOLEYS
6	CHRISTMAS EVE	27	McFADDENS REEL	48	CROWLEYS - DREAME	113	HIGH LEVEL
7	YELLOW TINKER	28	PIGEON ON THE GATE	49	St·COLLUMBUS	114	QUARELSOME PIPER
8	BUCKS OF ORANMORE	29	LAURLE BUSH	50	HUMOURS OF SCARRIFF	115	BANTRY BAY -
9	REEL OF BOGIE	30	KILLEBEG HOUSE	51	SÉAN SA CEÓ - 1 - 2 -	116	THREE SEA CAPTAINS
10	KITTYS GONE A·MILKING	31	THE·HIGH·REEL	52	THE LEA OF MULLINGAR	117	HUMOURS OF·BANDON
11	FLAX IN BLOOM	32	THE MOUNTAIN - TOP - REEL	53	LADY·ON·THE ISLAND	118	MAGGIE BROWN
12	DOGS·AMONG THE BUSHES	33	THE PEELERS JACKET	54	McCLOWEDS McLOEDS·REEL	119	GARDEN OF DAISIES
13	THE SAILORS JACKET.	34	LUCY·CAMPBELL	55	MOLLY WHAT AIL'S·YOU	120	DRUNKEN SAILOR -
14	MASTER McDERMOTS	35	THE·JOLLY TINKER	56	~~THE~~		ROYAL OAK· OR ROAD TO RIO -
15	HUMOURS OF LISADELL	36	THE MAID OF MOUNT CISCO	57	OUGHERIM - OR- KELLYS REEL		X
16	EILEEN CURRA	37	BUNKER HILL	58	BONNY KATE ~~~~		X
17	THE PUCH BOWL	38	THE·TEMPLE HOUSE				master Crowleys №1		X
18	BALLINASLOE - FAIR -	39	KATEYS WEDDING				-122-		X
19	BUCHE OF KEYS	40	PADDY RYANS DREAME				the Dawn -123-		X
20	ASH PLANT	41	FAREWELL TO IRELAND						X
21	TRIM THE VELVET	42	THE BEAUTY - SPOT -						X

THE BUNCH OF KEYS By Ted Furey

from John Doran 1933 Dublin

had Not Got Enought of Paper to finish the New Setting

(20) —"— THE ASH PLANT arranged By ted Furey —

from Pat mcnulty Scotland 1964 — Piper

ACADEMY

187

→ --the Lark - or -
Arranged By Ted Furey

I THE. LASS. ON. THE... STRAND.
74
P mcgrath + athboy Co Westmeath 1957

Furey

SUNRISE.
THE NEW YORK JIG
75
T. oHanlon gorey Co wexford 1960
Arranged By Ted Furey

Furey

THE PIPER O THE HOBB
OR THE CRICKET -
The LITTLE PEOPLES PIPER -
76
Phil griffitts Co Cavan. 1936
Arranged By Ted Furey

ACADEMY
MANUSCRIPT

Called By Some the Little Peoples Piper Ted Furey

188

THE CATS TROT TO THE CHILDS SAUSPAN --

92

GANDOR AT THE PRATTIE HOLE   arranged By Ted Furey
GANDOR AT THE [~~PRATTIE~~] HOLE. John Kelly Dublin 1963 --

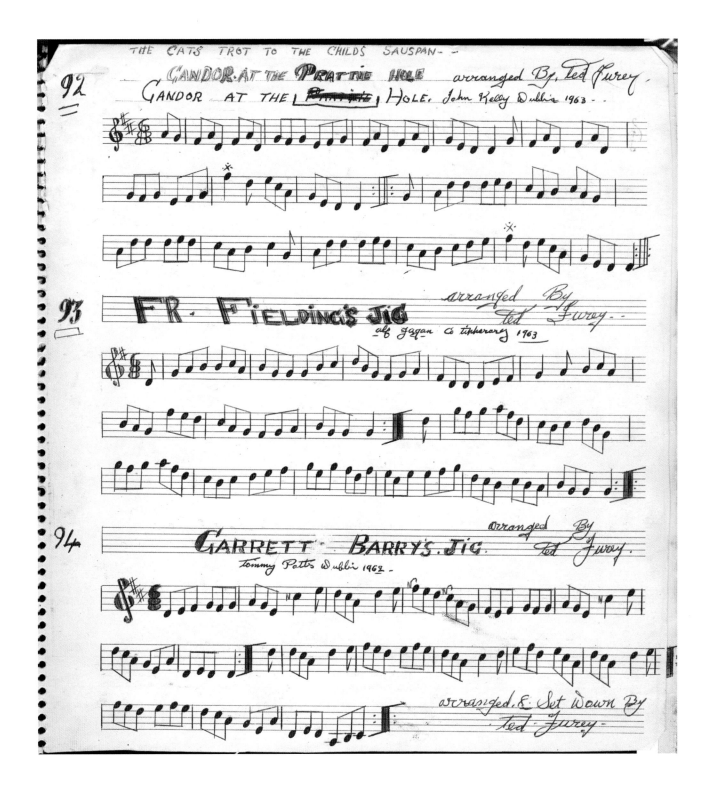

93

FR. FIELDING'S JIG   arranged By Ted Furey --
alf Gagan Co tipperary 1963

94

GARRETT BARRY'S JIG.   arranged By Ted Furey.
Tommy Potts Dublin 1962 --

arranged & Set down By Ted Furey --

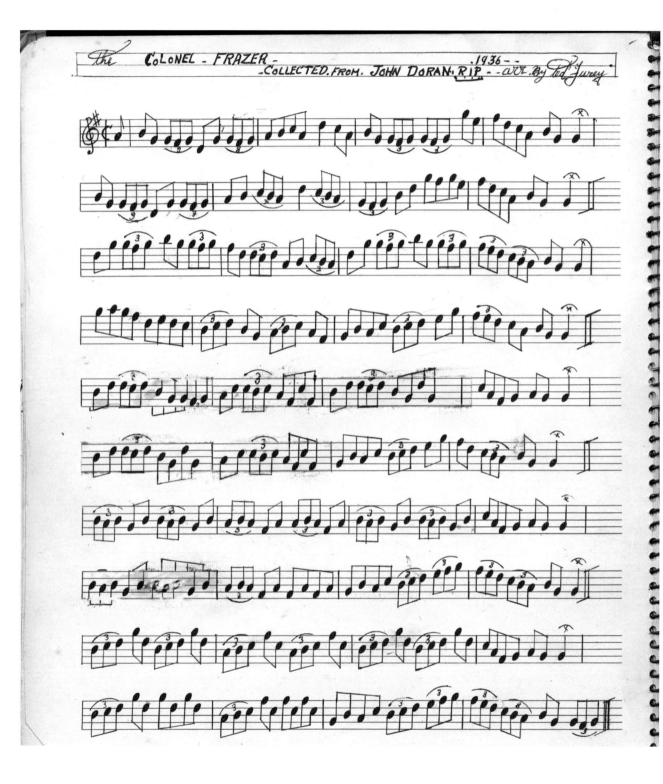

The COLONEL - FRAZER -
-COLLECTED.FROM. JOHN DORAN. RIP - arr. By Ted Furey.
.1936 - -

References

Bibliography

Brown, P. (2009) *Willie Clancy The Gold Ring. Uilleann Piping from County Clare*. RTÉ a T276 CD

Donegal Democrat, 1st. February, 1980)

Falsey, M. (22nd July, 1984), *Michael Falsey*, An Píobaire, Na Píobairí Uilleann, Dublin

Feldman, A. O'Doherty, E.(1979) *The Northern Fiddler*. Blackstaff Press Ltd, Belfast

Fiddler on the Road (1972) UTV, Belfast.

Gaynor, J. (September 24th 2002), Galway Advertiser, Galway

Gaynor, J. (September 24th, 2002) The Connacht Sentinel,

MacAoidh, C. (1994) *Between the Jigs and the Reels,* Drumlin Publications,

McCaffery, J. (12th June, 1961) *My Name is Cash the Piper*, Irish Press, 1961. Reproduced in Treoir, Comhaltas Ceoltóirí Éireann,

Mitchell, P. (1999) The Seán Reid Society Journal. Volume 1. March 1999. 1.1.12 *Rhythm & structure in Irish traditional dance music –* Part 1.The double jig as played on the Irish pipes. P 6

O'Neill, Capt. F. *Irish Minstrels and Musicians*, (1913), Chicago, Regan Printing House,

O'Toole, L. (2006) *The Humours of Planxty*. Hodden Headline, Dublin. pps 21-24

Touhy, D. and O hAodha M.(2008) *Postcolonial Artist, Johnny Doran and Irish Travellers' Tradition*, Cambridge Scholars Publishing. Newcastle. p78.

Van Diij, R. (1995) An Píobaire, Volume 4, Issue10

M'Fomhair/D'Fomhair, 1969, Dublin.

Williams, D. (1985) Strath 2, Uimhir 26, Iúil 1985 Na Píobairí Uilleann

Discography

Dermot McLaughlin, (1996) *Traditional Music from Donegal. John Doherty*. Ceirníní Cladaigh.

Doran, F. (1976) *The Last of the Traveling (sic) Pipers*. Topic: 12T288.

Evans, Alun. (1996) *The Floating Bow; Traditional Fiddle Music from Donegal*. John Doherty. Claddagh Records Ltd. Dublin

Finbar and Eddie Furey, *Finbar and Eddie Furey*, Transatlantic Records, TRA 168, (1968)

Finbar and Eddie Furey, *The Lonesome Boatman*, Transatlantic Records, TRA 191 (1969)

John and Simon Doherty, The Sailor's Trip, (1975) FTX-074. Topic Records Ltd., London

John Doherty *Bundle and Go - John Doherty - Master Fiddler of Donegal* - Topic 1984

Johnny and Felix Doran , (2008), *Traveller Piper, A Celebration of the Irish Traveller Tradition of Johnny and Felix Doran*, DVD. Na Píobairí Uilleann, Dublin.

Johnny Doherty, Bundle and Go. Topic 12TS 398; (1980) Green Linnet GLCD 3077; 1993

Johnny Doherty - Taisce - The Celebrated Recordings - Gael Linn 1977

Johnny Doherty, The Star of Donegal (1975) Ftx-075 Topic Records Ltd., London

Michael and Johnny Doherty, The Flowers of Edinburgh (1975),FTX-073

Shane MacGowan and the Popes (17th October 1994). *The Snake* (original release) - 4509-98104-2 (ZTT Records)

The Chieftains, *The Chieftains 2* (1969) Claddagh/Atlantic 83322-2, 2000. Reissue of Claddagh CC7, 1969. Recorded Apr. 1969 in Edinburgh.

The Donegal Fiddle - RTE CD

The Fureys, *The Fureys Sing Chaplin*, Brud Records, 2002.

The Raineys, *The Raineys,*(2007) Pavee Point Travellers' Centre, Dublin

Web Resources

Conroy, A. (1994) *An Píobaire*, Na Píobairí Uilleann, Dublin
Fergus Russell, ,(2007) *The Pat Rainey Song*. Dublin
Finbar Furey, (June 20th 2007) Interview RadioIrish.com, http://www.youtube.com/watch?v=-6Uk-yE0jss
http://comhaltas.ie/blog/post/johnny_doherty/.
http://donegalfiddlemusic.ie/musicallandscape.htm
http://encarta.msn.com/
http://folktrax-archive.org/menus/cassprogs/273.htm
http://www.encyclopedia.com/doc/1G2-3495900031.html Author unknown
http://www.myspace.com/johndoherty19
http://www.reocities.com/Athens/6464/tnf.html
http://www.seanreidsociety.org
Johnny Doherty. *Johnny Doherty*. Comhaltas Ceoltóirí Éireann, CL10
Kieran O'Kelly. 24-AUG-1993 Discussion Forum https://listserv.heanet.ie/cgi-bin/wa?A2=ind9309&L=IRTRAD-L&T=0&P=1123
Lynat, M. (2001) *The Raineys of the Road*. Connemara Community Radio, Ita Kane.
Mickey Doherty, *The Gravel Walks* (Comhairle Bhéaloideas Éireann, CBE 002).
Ochs, B. (1995) An Píobaire, Vol. 3, Issue 24, Na Píobairí Uilleann, Dublin
Paul McCann, (2005), *A Tribute to the Late Paul Furey* http://www.abctales.com/node/502607
Rochford, M. (1988), An Píobaire, Issue 2, No.43 15 October 1988, Templemore Tionól, Liam McNulty

Interviews

Cherry, R, (Friday,4 June, 2010) telephone Interview with Tommy Fegan, re John Doherty.
Doran, (April 24th 2009) Interview by Tommy Fegan and Oliver O'Connell, Doran Tionól, ,Bellbridge Hotel, Spanish Point, Co Clare-
Doran, M Senior. (December 5th, 2009) Interview with Tommy Fegan and Oliver O'Connell. Manchester.
Doran, M. Snr (May 18th, 2010). Telephone interview with Tommy Fegan.
Doran, M. Snr. (December 5th, 2009) Interview with Tommy Fegan and Oliver O'Connell. Manchester.
Doyle, Simon. (Manchester, October, 2010), interview by Tommy Fegan and Oliver O'Connell.
Dundon, W. (June, 2010) interview, by Tommy Fegan, Railway Bar, Newry.
Finbar Furey. F. (Friday 31, July 2009). Interview, Tommy Fegan and Oliver O'Connell. Spawell Hotel, Dublin.
Furey, Finbar and Martin, (Sunday 21st March, 2010), *Miriam Meets*. Miriam O'Callaghan, RTÉ Radio 1.
Gaffney, C. (May 21, 2009, & January 18, 2010), Interviews with Tommy Fegan, Tara Education Centre ,Dundalk,Nan Doran, Eileen.
Gaynor. C. (May 6th, 2009) Interview with Tommy Fegan. Co Louth VEC Travelers' Education Centre, Dundalk.
Kieran, R. (4th Feburary, 2010) Interview with Tommy Fegan, Canal Court Hotel, Newry.
Sands, T. (Dec.3rd, 2009) Interview : Tommy Fegan, Railway Bar, Newry.
Traveller Piper, (2008) *A Celebration of the Irish Traveller Tradition of Johnny and Felix Doran*, DVD. Na Píobairí Uilleann, Dublin.